T0368737

WorkBook

To
Reinvent Sales Process

For Information Technology Salespeople

Author: Ben Yan

Level 1 – The Fundamentals

It is all in the Qualifying Process.
"Increase Long Term Revenues for Technology Products
& Services Companies"
A HOW-TO book with step by step guides

Order this book online at www.trafford.com
or email orders@trafford.com

Most Trafford titles are also available at major online book retailers.

Note for Librarians: A cataloguing record for this book is available from Library
and Archives Canada at www.collectionscanada.ca/amicus/index-e.html

Printed in Victoria, BC, Canada.

ISBN: 978-1-4251-3796-0 (sc)

*We at Trafford believe that it is the responsibility of us all, as both individuals and corporations,
to make choices that are environmentally and socially sound. You, in turn, are supporting this
responsible conduct each time you purchase a Trafford book, or make use of our publishing services.
To find out how you are helping, please visit www.trafford.com/responsiblepublishing.html*

*Our mission is to efficiently provide the world's finest, most comprehensive book publishing
service, enabling every author to experience success. To find out how to publish your book, your
way, and have it available worldwide, visit us online at www.trafford.com*

Trafford rev.

 www.trafford.com

North America & international
toll-free: 1 888 232 4444 (USA & Canada)
phone: 250 383 6864 ♦ fax: 250 383 6804 ♦ email: info@trafford.com

The United Kingdom & Europe
phone: +44 (0)1865 487 395 ♦ local rate: 0845 230 9601
facsimile: +44 (0)1865 481 507 ♦ email: info.uk@trafford.com

What people say about the "Reinvent Sales Process Workbook?"

"No matter where you are in your sales career, Ben will guide you to better relations with your clients and lead you to having clients-for-life. *Reinvent Sales Process* is your personal strategic sales plan. Explore Client Buying Cycle with a sales visionary and have the tools to facilitate positive change."

Diverse, creative and innovative! *Reinvent Sales Process for IT* will become THE source book for a client-centric win-win. The focus is on understanding the prospect and how to turn them into long term clients. Decades of experience have been crafted into helpful hints, worksheets and focus.

Roger Harmston
Empower Management Inc.

"Ben has definitely captured all accelerators in terms of sales intelligence gathering, analysis, positioning, and focus. If sales managers were to utilize his approach and methodology, they empower their sales people to build a business plan and execute against that plan. His methodology is as much for management as it is for the sales reps when regular process of coaching and mentoring is in place."

Andrey Federoff,
Channel Manager, Alcatel-Lucent Canada.

"I am very impressed about the fresh approach to the sales process. Overall I am impressed and find it informative and insightful. In the "professional sales process", there is the need for more in-depth acceptances of technology to help in the sales process. Most Account Executives are still stuck in a mode of doing many of tasks manually and have not adopted the benefits of technology to advance our sales efforts. Technology solution, based on a systematic sales process methodology, will provide effective allocation of investment of time and resources."

Terry Zimmel
HP Printer, Davison

"This WorkBook is a good reference material for Ben's training course for people starting their sales career. With the inclusion of worksheets, Ben has outlined his methodology in a simple, easy to follow format. It is a solid refresher for veteran sales professionals."

Mike Volker
Industry Liaison Officer
Simon Fraser University

"There is always a need for great sales tools and advice as sales truly takes a bit of psychology, a bit of charm, and a systematic process. Ben has been able to use his years of experience and wisdom to provide a mix of all of those into a useful workbook for those tasked with building businesses and meeting quotas!"

Caroline Lewko,
CEO
Wireless Industry Partnership (WIP)
www.wipconnector.com

"The scientific, psychological and practical methodology makes it very comprehensive and guarantees an on-going usefulness of the materials. I also liked the interactive workshop approach, because that makes it immediately relevant for IT sales professionals and it seals the newly acquired knowledge into a valuable habit.

You have addressed all aspects of the sales cycle and together with the additional Programs, you have created a proven and valuable methodology that could revolutionize the hi-tech sales environment. Your methodology could be the pivotal factor that either makes the IT company successful, or if old approaches are followed, makes it obsolete. I would recommend it to all IT and hi-tech companies that want to differentiate and prosper in the new economy."

Madleine M. Rab
Executive Vice President
Citizen Bank

"The book definitely belies your extensive sales experience in the tech sector as it comes across as clear, pragmatic and action oriented. The worksheets and tables sprinkled throughout the text compel the reader to tie the reading back to their specific circumstance - something that will undoubtedly magnify its impact. I found the structure easy to follow as it flowed logically from The Pipeline to The Buying Process to Qualifying. There is little doubt that any sales person that follows the process and techniques outlined in your book will experience significant success. I have certainly made note of several new ideas that I plan to incorporate into our sales efforts."

Axel Christiansen, CFA
Investment Manager
VanCity Credit Union

"I really liked Ben's practical approach with worksheets and steps to work through to reinforce the learning. Another important point is that it would be a good way for an experienced sales person to take a new, refreshed approach to their work."

Dorothy Lowrie
Special Project Leader
Hewlett Packard Company

"Reinvent Sales Process for Information Technology Sector is a methodology everyone involved in selling technology products and services should internalize. Ben's first-hand knowledge of complex sales cycles and his access to research of how to effectively influence people's behaviour is critical information for all those whose job it is to close business and maintain long-term relationships with their customers."

James Wing
Sales Manager
Silect Software Inc
www.Silect.com

"Ben's sales methodology drills down the focus of sales staff to its market. It is simple and easy to adopt. Whether it is used by a certified instructor in a workshop setting, or if it is used in a self-study setting, the material and its exercises are field-tested and proven which will provide valuable direction to junior and senior sales staff in an easy to read and understand format."

Gary Patsey
President
EnTel Communications Inc

"Ben has leveraged his many years of experience and success to provide an ensemble of techniques and approaches that can help you to increase sales and improve your sales time to peak effectiveness. Selling is a blend of science, art and intuition. Intuition will come with experience; Ben provides some strong science tools and timely examples of the art."

Michael Kerr
Channel Manager
EMC Inc

"This book contains "Tools for Success", from finding the right clients, understanding challenges they face and coming up with the solutions needed. If you are selling in the technology industry and becoming a success is a goal for you, add this to your must read list."

Amber Ogilvie
Editor
24 Hours Publications

"Bottom line is I will be buying the books for my sales teams. Ben has achieved and exceeded this Goal of the Book that serves as training material at workshops and self-study ...excellent execution. It is very easy to read and comprehend and a huge RETAINMENT factor on the steps and cycles."

Mitch Poirier
President & CEO
Tix Systems Inc
Ottawa

"This book is an excellent training aid for building high performance sales teams. It summarizes complex sales models logically, it distils large amount of information into digestible modules, and it reinforces the learning with practical tools. I will highly recommend this to companies looking for a simple but effective way to improve their sales practice."

Claudia Ng
President
Fatport Wireless Inc

"Reinvent Sales Process" is presented in an easy to read style. Ben wrote it as a sales 'primer' yet it describes ALL the tools needed to be successful in sales in a manner that is easily understood and Ben made a "how to" book enjoyable. I welcomed the opportunity to use the work sheets and answer the questions throughout the book. The book elevates the sales role in a corporation from being a 'black art' to scientific precision. This book is ideally suited to become the training primer for a new sales rep, and it is a strategic sales planning and reporting toll for their sales managers."

Bill McLean
VP Business Development
MetroFibreWerx Inc

"This is a valuable tool for the mid-level technical sales professional as well as a beacon to guide entry-level sales people into the sales realm. Mr. Yan has uniquely blended savory sales-jargon, brilliant strategies with enough humor and real life situations so it immediately becomes a delightful, informative diversion from generic "tactical sales skill books". This study guide format encourages compartmentalized individual or group training and upgrading venues. It gives the author a legitimate title of "Mentor".

Dan Bouillet
Co-founder
GT Group Telecom

"This book is actually one of the very few I know which brings an efficient Sales methodology which can apply for small and large Deals and can be very easily implemented to any Sales Force within any company.

I strongly recommend reading this book and trying this methodology which according to my professional Experience can apply to any IT Business activity."

Bertrand COLLONGY
Former Country Manager, HP EMEA
(Europe, Middle East and Africa HP3000 Sales & Marketing Manager)
CEO of 2 IT Companies in FRANCE

Contents

Acknowledgements

When I decided to write this workbook, it was a daunting experience. Without the help and encouragement from my colleagues and close friends, this would not have happened. Many have offered comments and written their reviews even before it was published.

My special thanks to Andrey Federoff, Channel Manager of Alcatel-Lucent * Fred Shaw, Regional Manager of Ingram Micro * Geoff Routledge of Canfor Forest Products * Roger Harmston of Empower Management * Geoff Kereluik, Sr. VP of Hewlett Packard * Bill Davis, VP of Sales HP Western Region * Dorothy Lowry, Solution Director of HP * Terry Zimmel, HP Imaging Division * George Vesnaver, Global Manager, Software division of HP * Michael Kerr, Channel Director of EMC * Mitch Poirier, CEO of Tix Systems Inc * Tom Rutledge of Systems Consortium International * Bertrand Collongy, CEO of Lye Communications in Lyon, France * Mike Volker, Simon Fraser University Industry Liaison Officer * Benny Cifelli, Dir of sales of NetApp *, Mike Rostad, Dir of BC Government Business Unit of Telus Communications * Stacy Kusiak, Faculty of Commerce, University of Victoria, Jas Sahota, EMC, Claudia Ng, Infowave Systems Inc * Tom Teixerira, Sr VP of Open Solutions Inc * Steve Cuccione, Director of Education Business Unit of IBM, Brad Neufeld, VP Sales of Carmanah * Gary Patsey, President of Entel Communications * Bill McLean, President of MetroFibreWerx Inc * Caroline Lewko, CEO of WIP (Wireless Partnership) Inc * Madeleine Rabb, VP and GM of Bell Canada, 2008 Olympics enterprise * Amber Ogilvie, Publisher of 24 Hrs Publication * Paul Commessotti, Country Manager of Checkpoint Inc.

I want to extend a very special thank you to Mike Volker, Industry Liaison Officer of Simon Fraser University, a very dear friend and mentor to many technology entrepreneurs, for his time and the effort spent in reviewing and editing the workbook. My deepest appreciation to Dan Bouillet, Co-Founder of GT Group Telecom;

Jas Sahota, Channel Manager of EMC Corp; Mitch Poirier, VP of Zentra; Stacy Kuiack, Business Leader of University of Victoria, Bertram Collongy, President of Lys Informatique in France for their coaching, comments, and editing through the journey of writing of this workbook to reinvent the sales process for sales professionals in the information technology industry.

Introduction

The purpose of this workbook is to present a concise, simple sales process for the information technology industry. It is s a step by step approach for building your own pipeline, your account management strategy, and your own future and success as a sales professional. Your ultimate goal would be to internalize this simple process so that you can focus on your client's needs and benefits.

It is my intention to help you to adopt a simple repeatable sales process that your subconscious mind can absorb in an immersion manner. When you internalize this simple process in an organized fashion, you are half way there. Once you follow the instructions and complete your assignment at the end of each section, you will have internalized this reinvented sales process.

This workbook is derived from many sales training camps, courses and experiences in my career. By internalizing this simple process, you can apply the proven tools to different sales situations. You should blend in your personality, character and your own style with this process. There are numerous triggering questions to intrigue your thought process. You can use the tools to analyze and measure your own progress, and evaluate your own level of adoption at the end of each section. This process is so simple that you can gauge your own progress and reinforce your internalization process.

Many sales professionals are in constant pursuit of that silver bullet in selling, especially when their sales results suffer in economic downturns. In our years of searching, we found no such prescription for silver bullets. However, if you can internalize a simple, repeatable sales process, you are half way there. With regular consistent coaching from a mentor, you will earn your stripes in your sales career. This is the goal of this workbook.

Although it is worded around the technology industry, you will find these same basic principals effective in many other industry sectors. I have integrated the strategic process with a focus on the behavioral buying patterns and decision making process of your prospects in your target market. When I designed the structure of this workbook, it was aimed at study groups and also as a self-study guide. It will become your second nature when you receive regular coaching from a mentor. This will assist you to reinvent the sales process for your lifelong benefit.

Practice is part of the internalization process of our subconscious mind. Training is only the beginning of this internalization process. If you treat a workshop or training program as the destination, you are missing the most exciting journey of the sales profession. Bottom line --- there is no silver bullet and selling is an ongoing journey of improvement.

Most sales training books focus on techniques and methodology, rather than on the process of internalization. You learn consciously and you will acquire the skills by immersion. You live and breathe your sales profession and perform naturally and flawlessly when your subconscious mind does the work.

My goal is to contribute my experiences and the knowledge that I have developed and accumulated over the past few decades. I have had the good fortune to work alongside many sales professionals and associates. I strongly advise you to adopt good working habits early in your career, and adhere to a high level of professional ethical conduct for a satisfying and successful life.

Learning a new foreign language, driving an automobile, and acquiring a new golf swing are several examples of learning new skills. How much do you retain after a class or a lesson? Without doing the assignments, or regular practice, you will lose the information within a short period of time. According to one university study, students lose about 30% of classroom information the minute they walk out of the classroom. So you have to train your conscious mind to learn new skills. You must practice and practice until you accumulate our mileages and experiences. Eventually, your newly acquired skills become your second nature and you find yourself in the autopilot mode. You must be mindful not to develop bad habits and start with the right skills and information in your routines. Do not give up on your new-found methodology before your subconscious mind gives you the autopilot certificate. Commit to a simple, repeatable, proven methodology and stay with it until you have internalized the process.

Another important aspect of a successful sales process is continual awareness & upgrading after your internalization of the skills and process.

As a creature of habit, you have to hone your skills so it becomes second nature to you. When you are in an autopilot mode, your subconscious mind takes over.

You know from past experience that upon completion of a sales training course, you may apply it for 2 weeks, and habitually switch back to your old methods. The reason is simple. Your subconscious mind has a legacy to deal with whenever you introduce a new method. You have to change those old habits and internalize new skills. Another key is to stay with a process that is proven, repeatable, and easy to be internalized. Get into an autopilot state within a short period of time with dedicated coaching. Coaching by a mentor will accelerate the growth of your career. Most sales managers are successful salespeople, yet they may not have time to be coaches or mentors. Coaching requires time and a different skill set, so it may be profitable to seek outside resources.

How this WorkBook is structured. How you can benefit from the book.

This is a practical Workbook to help you to adopt a simple, proven, repeatable sales process. It consists of real life success stories, applications and professional skill-sets designed from my boot camp workshops and seminars. Use it as a workbook to shape and formulate your personal sales plan. Follow your plan, work at it, and experience the results. You will find this proven method also applies to most sales situations, regardless of industry or product.

A side benefit of working efficiently with this blue print is work life balance. Whether you are an entrepreneur sales agent, a value-added reseller, or a major manufacturer representative, you are essentially an independent business person. Your work life balance style provides you with a healthy growth environment.

When you work through the assignments, keep your business practice in your mind. Think about how to apply each assignment in your day to day practice. Upon completion of this WorkBook, you would have developed your own plan of action, personal reviews, measurement metrics, and a set of tools that you can immediately use in the field. By then, you would have a much better understanding of the status of your operation.

As you read through the pages of this WorkBook, you are virtually attending one of my live workshops. Invest your time, complete the assignments and internalize the process.

There are Four Parts that detail the fundamentals of this simple sales process. As you set your own pace and complete the assignments you are gradually building your own Strategic Personal Plan.

Part I:	The Pipeline
Part II:	Stages of Buying Cycle
Part III:	Qualification Process
Part IV:	Sales Activities Management

Assignments are designed to trigger your thought process. You can apply your learned skill to your own sales situations and opportunities immediately. Tips are given through the "triggering" question format. These questions help you in your assignment and your professional practice. You will also learn questioning skills to enhance your fact finding capability. Another important skill is your listening skill. You have to practice that with your coach. Your listening skill will help you in building your confidence and credibility with your prospect.

The pinnacle of your learning is internalization. Learning is an ongoing process for which you must invest time and effort. Internalization does not happen after a 2-day boot camp event. You must continue to solicit coaching from a mentor who will recognize and appreciate the sales accelerators outlined in this Reinvent Sales Process.

Part I - The Pipeline

This is your entry point to building a successful sales career. Your Pipeline is your target market. It is your territory, your turf, your reservoir of prospects, your battlefield, war zone and your long term bank account. This chapter helps you to identify and understand your prospects. You define your own target market scientifically through your own strength, expertise and vertical market, along with the available support infrastructure from your organization.

Before the personal computer was invented in the 80's, sales people used 3"x5" index cards to record their prospects' information. They used recipe boxes as their repository of prospects. Combining the recipe box and a calendar, they had the basic tools to work with. This recipe box is your Pipeline. This historic lesson teaches you about the importance of keeping a repository of prospects in one safe place. You can refer to them whenever and wherever you need them.

Who should be included in this "recipe box"? How do you select these prospects? This recipe box is your prospect database. It helps you to become more efficient and be able to synchronize with your company's marketing plan. This is the foundation of your success. It is your base to achieve your overall goals and objectives. You should work through the worksheets and file them in a 3-ring binder. This is the home base of your personal sales plan. You can review and measure your progress with quantifiable results.

Worksheets are provided to you in the WorkBook. These useful tools will guide you to identify the "ideal" prospects that you want as clients. These clients have technology requirements that your company can deliver. You then work through the process of listing, and identifying all their challenges. A series of suggestions and questions helps you along in this process. During this process, you do not have to think of your solution's fit as yet. When you zero in on specific prospect requirement, you will then match their challenges (business pains) with your solutions. When you drill down on your solution deliverables, you will uncover your own niche, your expertise and the suitable vertical market segment. These Worksheets and examples will help you to fully internalize this target segment.

You will be given the "recipe", a step-by-step approach for using these Worksheets. They are very simple to use. You can apply this tool in your daily operation immediately.

The next stage is to understand and qualify your prospects. We give you a list of questions that trigger your thought process to understand your prospect in a concise manner. By the end of each assignment, you have a better picture of your vertical market landscape.

After you define your Pipeline's parameters, you then proceed to set your own rules of engagement. Make a quick decision in qualifying these prospect --- Rule them in or out, at this early stage of Qualification. It saves you valuable time and energy down the road. When you establish your Pipeline Parameter Statement, it becomes your mission statement in your personal sales plan. This chapter also instructs you on where to find high quality prospects.

Part II - Buying Cycle

Your prospect exhibits certain buying behavior and follows a decision making process. However, these are dynamic stages. Use the criteria in the WorkBook as your guideline. Plan your own activities and categorize your prospect to these stages of buying accordingly. It helps you to allocate necessary resources, such as your time and your support team's resources. Perform the right activities at the right stage of the buying cycle. Develop your daily, weekly, monthly and yearly work plan. You are on course to establish your model of operational efficiency. You can delegate some of the tasks to your subordinates if possible. This is a scientific and systematic model to allocate your valuable resources.

For example: Doing a proposal at the wrong time wastes resources, especially if you don't know the stage of their buying cycle. It is your job to motivate them through their buying cycle by constant qualification. What to do and how you do it adds credibility in building a trusting relationship with your prospects. When you become a trusted advisor to your prospect, you become the ultimate sales professional.

This model proves how people embrace new technologies and their process of procurement. These Stages are:

1. Indifferent,
2. Interested,
3. Qualified,
4. Committed,
5. Closed/Sold.

You learn how to classify your prospects based on their Buying Cycle. At the end of every encounter, you evaluate and realign your prospects using your Qualification ScoreCard. When you have a clear picture of their Buying Cycle, you can focus your energy and allocate your team resources in the most effective manner. You can organize your sales activity in your sales operation in a timely manner.

In this WorkBook, you learn how to scientifically quantify these Stages of Buying Cycle – The Qualifying Process.

Part III - Qualifying Process

In the technology industry, manufacturers introduce new products with a shortened life cycle compared to a decade ago. You must be aware of the product life cycle and match them with your prospect's buying cycle, your target market and the buying cycle of your target clients. This section presents you with several useful motivation keys to accelerate your prospects from one Stage of Buying Cycle to the next. You know your ultimate goal is to accelerate this process to a *Closed/Sold* stage:

- Solution Matching (Product Alignment)
- Circle of Influence (Players)
- Time line & milestones (Time Frame), and
- Funding (Approved Budgets).

Use the *Qualification ScoreCard* to analyze scientifically and evaluate the Stages of Buying Cycle of your prospect. This is an objective evaluation of your prospect's buying cycle. It makes your life easy and your sales process simple and systematic. *The Qualification Questionnaire guides you through this process of completing the Qualification ScoreCard.* Once you complete the assignment, you can design your own Qualification Questionnaire to meet your special market needs. When you internalize these answers, you come to the next level. Internalize a minimum of

FIVE different ways to ask each question to cover the majority of sales situations. This is a very systematic step by step approach and a recipe approach to populate the Scorecard. It is adaptable in all your prospects' environments.

This section coaches you on how to refine your questioning, listening and interpersonal skills. Many important tips and examples are given. We strongly suggest that you spend appropriate time to cultivate the qualifying questions provided. Following the logical step by step approach, you can populate the Scorecard with all relevant information for action.

When you work through each assignment, you accumulate a repository of qualifying questions. You can "position" your prospect into the right stage of his Buying Cycle.

A Qualification Scorecard Matrix is the summary of all Qualifying Keys and automatically provides you with the scientific summary of the Stage of Buying Cycle. When you use this tool with each prospect in your sales situations, you will instantly improve your results in your target market. You must constantly update this Qualification Scorecard as it is designed as a working document and a roadmap, to manage the prospect in the Pipeline.

Part IV - Sales Activities Management

How your prospect accepts new ideas and new technology is very crucial in the Buying Cycle. All assignments are designed to help you to develop your own set of criteria and to manage your own sales activities in the territory.

These activities are crucial to your selling effort, marketing events, business development activities, customer service and long-term customer relationship efforts. It requires diligent work in your daily operation. When you adopt a sales process, you must put it in practice. You will eventually internalize this "Reinvent Sales

Process Methodology". This is neither a canned nor a robotic approach. Rather, it is a proven natural path to success.

Your objective is to motivate your prospect to move to the next level of their buying cycle. Your responsibility is to seamlessly accelerate the buying process of your prospect so they become your lifelong customer.

The sales process is dynamic. If you missed one opportunity, don't be discouraged. You know that you cannot sell to everybody. It is important to learn how to deal with losses and manage the emotional aspect of a failure. Learn from the experience and be a better sales person.

Select a simple process. Ingrain it, practice and seek coaching. Never stop learning, and fine tune your newly acquired skill set.

Part I - The Pipeline

The Pipeline - The Target Market

Introduction

This is the foundation of your business practice. When you receive your revenue goals and objectives (sales quota) from your manager, you are tasked with a mission. Your company has articulated its business and marketing plans. Your personal sales plan is a subset of the overall marketing plan. Your job is to find the "ideal" prospect that has the business pain. It is your job to find them in your Pipeline.

You must first define the characteristic of your Pipeline. You can then drill down and focus your activities accordingly. This helps you to be more efficient and synchronizes with your company's marketing plan. This is your ultimate target market, the Pipeline.

The *Pipeline Qualification Worksheet* will guide you through this process. It lets you identify the "ideal" prospects with technology requirements that your company can deliver.

The following figure illustrates Your Pipeline. The horizontal arrow is time. When developing a business plan or a new marketing campaign, sales related activities start at the same place: Your Personal Sales Plan. The Business Plan therefore, is our starting point.

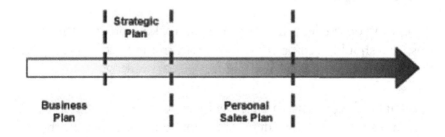

The business plan encompasses your overall vision, mission, strategy, goals and the objectives of your company. The sales plan is part of the overall business strategy. Your own sales plan is a subset

of the overall company's sales plan. You should design a personal
sales plan. This is your Mission and Assignment before you
embark on any engagement with prospects. In some cases, your
manager may have assigned a territory for you and provided you
with a guideline. It is your responsibility to focus on your Pipeline
if he hasn't done so. You must understand the overall goals
and objectives of the company's business plan, in particular the
marketing strategy of your company. If you are an entrepreneur,
you have do them all by yourself. The Strategic Plan outlines the
company's SWOT (Strength, Weakness, Opportunity and Threat),
Action Plan and milestones, projections and resource requirements
to succeed. A key component of the Marketing Plan is the
definition of your Target Market. The Target Market is a list
comprised of companies that you have identified as most likely to
have a demand for your products or services.

You must define the parameters of the Pipeline and develop your
own Personal Sales Plan before you begin to generate revenues.
By populating the Pipeline with prospects that are viable for
you to do business with, you exclude those prospects who are
not. In essence, you reduce your business development activities
significantly by focusing resources on the Pipeline. These prospects
are companies that meet your assigned responsibility and the
nature of your territory. If it is a vertical market such as health care,
you have your job carved out for you. It is your turn to focus your
time and energy.

Depending on the length of the decision making process, these
prospects should become your clients within the next two years.
They simply haven't said "Yes!" yet.

If you are selling to enterprise accounts, your prospects are
companies that meet your defined parameters. Ask yourself the
following question:

*"What are the qualifying parameters that I should include in my
Pipeline? "*

__Thought Triggering Hints:__ Consider the status of their companies. Are they a growing company in my vertical market? What type of companies do you want to do business with? Do you want to use the benchmark of size, number of employees, revenue, or the number of branches?

Allocation of your resources --- Time and Energy:

As professional sales people in the high tech sector, it is difficult to effectively service everyone. Use the guidelines in the following pages to zoom in on the parameters of your Pipeline so that you focus on a manageable and highly targeted list. This will save you a tremendous amount of time, energy and company resources.

It is important to refine the parameters of your Pipeline step by step. The worksheet included in this WorkBook will help you to clearly define your target market. Your Pipeline should consist of prospects that you want to work with. The key is to ensure that you will have a constant supply of qualified prospects in your Pipeline.

Upon completion, these worksheets will determine exactly with whom you will and will not do business with. It's also easier to develop a good relationship with someone who fits your definition of an "ideal" client when they have similar technology requirements that your company can deliver.

Examples of Prospects in Vertical Markets:

1. *Forestry: Revenue base, number of employees, remote branches, international offices, IT annual budget, profit/loss. Changes of government regulation that impacts IT infrastructure/ applications. (i) Softwood lumber, (ii) Environmental, safety, (iii) Foreign Manufacturing mills, (iv) Union changes.*

2. *Financial Sectors: Sarbanes-Oxley Regulation creates a new compliance application in their IT application.*

Define Your Company's Pipeline Parameters

In this section, you will learn how to develop your own Pipeline parameters. The objective is to rule-out the suspect very early in the game. It saves you time and resources. Rule them out when they don't meet your clearly defined criteria.

When your customer provides you with a referral, what should you do? What is the first question that comes to mind?

> *"With respect to my Pipeline, where do they fit?*
> *Should I rule-in or rule-out this prospect?"*

During one of your networking events, you collected a stack of business cards. Did you make any notes on the back of the business cards to help you remember and to screen them more effectively? It will help to jot down information as you meet with many people at these functions. Do it subtly and immediately after each conversation so you don't forget the information. The information helps you to rule-in or rule-out these potential prospects. Make it a habit of doing it next time when you are at such an event.

Do not automatically input all business cards into your contact management program. You should perform a screening process on all of them before you do so. The determining factor is whether they are even qualified to be included in your Pipeline. You make the judgment call to "Rule-In" or "Rule-Out", and you can design your own process. First, you must define the criteria of inclusion for your Pipeline database.

Your contact management software should store your existing clients, suppliers, alliance partners, prospects, etc. Your prospects should be labeled as such, awaiting your business development activities to work their magic. If you have the luxury of a separate database, you can insert them in a "Marketing Database". You can decide on the priority and the resource allocation accordingly.

Heads up!   *Your "Marketing Database" is a different list from your "Pipeline." Your Pipeline is filled with prospects, they just haven't said "Yes!" yet.*

General Pipeline Parameter

Location is a good starting point. If you are based in Phoenix, Arizona, selling information technology integration services that require multiple face-to-face meetings a year, then one of your Pipeline parameters would definitely be "location" --- the city of Phoenix and perhaps its suburbs. Depending on your clients' buying behaviour, you can adjust the criterion accordingly. For instance, your geographic parameter might be "the world" if you can satisfy your clients' needs via the Internet 24 hours a day.

Some points to consider:

▶ Are your clients comfortable not seeing you or any of your support team members at all? Once a year? Twice may be?

▶ Is your selling model a SWAT Project Team approach? For example, when you qualify the budget and your company is one of the few in the world that can do this type of project, you are automatically short-listed. You bring in your SWAT Team. This is a very specialized service, such as cleaning up an oil spill in Alaska

▶ Will they buy over the telephone or the Internet, or do they need to see you in person before they will sign a contract? Are there enough gross margins built into your solution to travel?

You should begin with a Pipeline that has focus, precisely defined parameters, and then expand them as you grow. Ask yourself, "How else can I narrow the parameters of my Pipeline so that I can concentrate on the cream of the crop that rises to the top?"

Example: *A large CRM software company recently stated on its website that it deals in the "small to mid-range" business market. They narrow their Pipeline by defining what that means on their website: "Small businesses are companies who are no more than 100 employees and revenues of no more than $25 million per annum. Medium sized* companies have 101 to 1000 employees with revenues up to $250 million." If you're bigger than that, they don't want to talk to you.

Example: *A computer hardware company wants to focus their Pipeline in the forestry industry. Their sweet spot is small and medium size pulp and paper mill operations. The employee count is about 250 people, revenue base $250 million, minimum 3 mills and within the Pacific Northwest Region. That's a narrow Pipeline. Their solution is a complete network infrastructure, server and disk storage, mill automation, and financials/ERP.*

General Pipeline Parameters

Fill in some of your company's Pipeline parameters that exist today, and add more as you complete this worksheet.

General Pipeline Parameters	Your Pipeline Parameters
1. Geographic territory: Countries are large. Consider specific states, provinces and cities. (How many visits do you need to promote your solution? The frequency has an impact on the selection of your location.)	
2. Size of company: By number of employees and by revenue. We recommend that you use both. (Employee counts impact IT infrastructure expenses. Revenue base gives you an idea if the company can afford the extra investment.) E.g. SMB: "small medium business". Go with the number of employees, which can give you an indication of IT infrastructure and network requirements.	
3. SIC (Standard Industry Code): Decide which industries you don't want to deal with. (Identifying your vertical in SIC code helps your data mining, EIS intelligence.)	
4. Ownership/corporate status: "SOHO", i.e. small office/home office, public, private, non-profit or government. (This factor is closely related to #2, Size of Company, and employee count.)	
5. Location of headquarters: Very important if your solution requires the ultimate authority of the CEO, president, CIO, or key decision makers.	

6. Years in business: For instance, you may not wish to do business with any company less than three years old. The only exception is if they are heavily financed.	
7. Fast growing companies: High tech, telecommunication, biotech, health, film, tourism, etc. (Understand the trend of their businesses. Biotech and health have long sales cycles due to multiple, bureaucratic processes.	
8. Title/position of individuals: We always start at the top. CEOs and presidents make decisions about who their long-term partners are.	
9. Stage of company: Start-up, capital acquisition, well-established going concerns, venture capitalist financing or IPO).	
10. Credit rating: Dunn & Bradstreet report or other assurances of liquidity.	
11. Anything else you can think of that will further narrow the parameters of your Pipeline even more?	

Narrow Your Pipeline Parameters Even More!

You must fine tune your Pipeline on a regular basis. This is called the "Zero-In Factor". When the economy is booming, the 80/20 rule applies. When the economy is taking a dive, the 90/10 rule applies. You must focus on quality prospects. You must also start working with your current customers proactively.

Assignment: Drill down further on defining your narrow Pipeline parameters even more. Add "specific" Pipeline parameters as they relate to each of your general parameters.

Helpful Hint: The CEO or president should be located in a city that falls within your "geographic" parameter if your sale requires eyeball-to-eyeball negotiations with the top decision maker. For example, you encounter a great company with the CEO in Seattle and you are located in Toronto. If you don't have the human resource in that city, or the financial resources to fly, then it falls outside the "geographic" parameter, and is excluded from further consideration.

Things to consider:

▶ **Companies that buy parallel products from other suppliers.** Look at different mergers and strategic alliances over the last few years like Microsoft and Fox Network.

▶ **Look for cross-marketing opportunities.**

▶ **Look for alliances** that sell to the same market segment.

▶ **Cross-Markets selling:** Oracle, Informix, SQL will sell their database solution to your prospect. Cisco will be selling their hardware into your vertical segment as well. Think, what is in it for them? Define an official program to work with these sales professionals.

▶ **Business-to-business (B2B) purchasers only,** not business-to-consumer (B2C).

▶ **Plans to grow:** This is your prospect's roadmap to grow their company. For example, upgrading software or hardware is a necessary planning step if they have an aggressive marketing plan or if they are in an acquisition mode. Serious prospects will have this information documented somewhere within the company. If they don't have their mandates in writing, you may not want them in your Pipeline. On the other hand, you may have the resources available to help them with this shortfall, which is an opportunity for you.

Working the Numbers Backwards

Drill down to narrow the scope of your Pipeline parameters further. First, with your current resources in mind, and using all of the parameters that you defined for your Pipeline, determine the number of prospects with whom you can build relationships with and turn them into happy Lifelong Customers over the next three years.

Objective: *You should have a manageable number of prospects to successfully build profitable and sustainable relationships.*

Major corporations have large marketing departments and sales forces; they have the resources allocated to handle large Pipelines. IBM, HP, Dell, and Cisco have invested significantly in marketing, pre-sales engineering support, channel distribution support and post sales customer services divisions. Their sales force focuses on account management and territory business development.

If you're an independent business or sales agent who is single-handedly responsible for 100% of your selling efforts including all of your advertising, marketing, proposal writing, prospecting, reviewing requests for proposals, conducting assessments and closing the deal, then think very carefully about how many prospects you can handle in your Pipeline at a given period of time. When you organize and prioritize your Pipeline activities, you are more productive with the same resources available. This is a very important factor to consider when you populate your Pipeline.

Your current Pipeline parameters may be too broad depending on your organization's support infrastructure. You may be able to develop a list of 10,000 prospects. But, is this number an unreasonable workload for you considering your current resources? Keep narrowing the parameters of your Pipeline, so you don't end up overwhelmed. You can pay attention to the prospects that you can service and give them the attention. Do not spread yourself too thin in your practice.

You can start with as many as 5,000 potential prospects in your Pipeline, or as few as 50. A tiny boutique 4-Partner law company ramps up their business as they win projects. They have very few resources so they deal strictly with the most senior decision makers within their expertise target market. They only need to close one deal a month to sustain their growth. They narrow their Pipeline parameters and decide who they would engage to do business with. You have to decide on how many prospects you can manage in your Pipeline and focus.

Concentrate on a specific, carefully targeted market. Clearly define your Pipeline parameters with your limited, yet tactical resources in mind.

Helpful Hint: Whether you start with 100, 1,000 or 100,000 potential clients in your Pipeline, they have to be the best 100, 1,000 or 100,000 potential clients that perfectly match your company's solutions and resources.

How to Ensure Success

Don't attract what you don't want. The following assignment gives you the opportunity to write down "what you don't want". Ruling out is very simple and easy to do.

Assignment: *Write down all the parameters that you do not want to target.*

_____

Example: Unprofitable companies. Companies with less than 50 employees.
_____

_____

_____

_____

_____

_____

_____

_____

_____

_____

"Pipeline Parameter Statement"

To ensure success, you need a *"Pipeline Parameter Statement."* This tool will help to attract lucrative referrals from your friends, clients, alliance partners and associates.

Being specific about whom you wish to attract makes it easier for people to help you.

Taking the data that you have developed using the worksheets, develop your Pipeline Parameter Statement by filling in the blanks:

"We help companies that are located in _____ , And are in these three industry sectors, (_____ , _____ , and _____); and are profitable to sustain a high rate of client retention."

Clearly communicate this sentence to your team so that they can attract high caliber prospects that can be best served by your company.

Tips: This is similar in nature to the mission statement in the company. All team members must internalize this statement so they can be more efficient in identifying prospects to place in the Pipeline.)

What are their business problems? Do they have any Business Pain? What challenges do your prospects have to deal with?

Your prospects buy products, services and integrated solutions to solve their business problems. They want your assurance of reliable, quality services because they want the peace of mind. Consider other business problems that they experience in their daily operation, such as cost cutting on long distance expenses, increasing their sales revenue, reducing unnecessary overtime workers, meeting new legislation of privacy act and managing multi-branch network security. Do not forget to think about the challenges they expect in the future, such as under performance of their current ERP (Enterprise Requirement Plan) application servers, email server, disk farm capacity limitation and web server.

CEOs, Presidents, CIOs, CFOs and operation managers encounter different business issues on a day-to-day, week-to-week, and year-to-year basis. These prospects have their unique, individual business challenges and responsibilities. CEOs have a different mandate than the CFO, yet their mandates overlap to create value for their shareholders. It is important to realize their mandates during this process.

Assignment: *List at least 10 potential challenges, business pains, business problems and number them.*

Thought Triggering Questions: *"Speed of technological change" is a challenge that many companies face. What is their attitude towards the role of technology in their business? What is their impact? What are the potential long term benefits if they adopt new technology to enhance the performance of their companies?*

Samples of Technology Solutions:

- *Evolution of VoIP technology is being adopted by the industry. Time saving, money savings for multiple branch operations, E-Commerce security management, Outsourcing, and managed services.*

Executive Positions	Challenges/Business Pain
CEO (Chief Executive Officer)	
COO (President)	
CFO (Chief Financial Officer)	
Project Manager	

Your Company's Solutions – What do you offer?

"Products" are tangible goods, like servers and network switches. "Services" are intangibles that form part of the "whole" product (Total Solution) you offer. If you are a management consulting service firm, your offerings of "Status Reports", "Research Project" or "Written Recommendations" are your product services. They are all solutions offered to your prospect to help them solve their business problems. In summary, your solutions are *deliverables* to your prospects.

Assignment: *List at least 10 products or services that you offer today.*

Examples of services/products:

1. *Consulting services*
2. *Network topology design*
3. *Internet security management*
4. *Cisco network integration*
5. *VoIP*
6. *Data management*
7. *Identity Management*
8. *Wireless network access point deployment*
9. *Oracle database management (DBA)*
10. *Internet appliance*
11. *Virtualization of storage, server (Storage Consolidation, server consolidation)*
12. *Wide Area Network optimization*

Priority	Solutions You Offer
1.	
2.	

Matching Problems with Solutions

Now you should have a list of your prospects' business problems and the list of products (solutions) you offer. Match them with as many of the appropriate solutions that would solve their particular problem.

Example (1): Challenge 1. Overtime at month end on payroll processing. Solution A. Automated payroll application

Example (2): Challenge 2. Critical Application Support. Solution B. 24-hour Non-Stop Help Desk Support

Challenge(Business Problems)	Solution You Offer
1. Overtime worker at month end on payroll processing	A. Automated payroll processing
2. Off hour critical application support	B. 24-hour Non-stop Help Desk Support

Assignment: *Match your solution offerings to the business problems of your prospect in the following table.*

Challenge(Business Problems)	Solution You Offer

Examination of Discovery (Fact Finding)

After you tabulate your findings of the business challenges of your prospect and your solution offerings, you should know if you have the right target market. Some of your solutions may not meet some of your prospects' challenges. This is the discovery of reality. If your solution offering is a match to solve your prospects' problems, you are on the right track.

If your discovery is not conclusive and does not confirm your expectation, you want to either refocus your resources to a different target market or re-package your solution to solve your prospect's business problems. This is a decision that you have to make to optimize your investment of time and resources.

Quite often, some of your prospects' problems cannot be solved with your current packaged solution set. Or, simply they are struggling with an incomplete, feeble solution that will not really solve their problem. You may want to rethink your solution packaging to meet their needs. You can also roll out a new whole product or bundle your existing offerings with a strategic partner's products. It is important that you offer a "whole" product instead of a perceived weak solution.

The possibilities to "under-promise and over-deliver" are endless, but first you have to understand the business problems and requirements of your prospects.

Thought Triggering Questions:

This is the time to examine the features, advantages, and benefits of your product offerings. Does your product solve the business problem for your prospect? Is it time to seriously revamp the solution set or bundle your service with other partners? Go back to your solution offerings and re-evaluate its marketing approach to your target market.

Example: *If you try to sell a "fat" client terminal to a prospect that is a centralized data centre shop, you are in trouble. When the whole market shifts to "thin" client architecture, you may wish to re-examine your product offering.*

Do you have an "Expertise"

You may specialize in a certain "vertical" market segment. For example, do you sell exclusively to the financial services sector and focus on banks, credit unions and financial planners because of your expertise and successful track record in this sector? These are the industries where you are personally or corporately perceived as an "expert." An expert is someone who has a deep understanding of his or her major industry focus and its unique challenges.

As a selling representative, you succeed when you match your education, expertise and vocabulary with an industry sector where there is a good fit. For instance, a former nurse may do well in the pharmaceutical industry. Their "expertise" could be heightened when they deal with people they like.

Assignment: *Write down all industry sectors that you consider yourself an expert in, or where you consider yourself as having a deep understanding of this "vertical." Then, place an asterisk (*) next to your top three expert industry sectors.*

Example: *Heavy Duty Equipment Manufacturing

Example: Financial Services

Example: Natural resources (mining, forestry, agriculture, fishery)

Example: Entertainment (video, audio, film, broadcast, music)

Example: Health Care, telecommunication, government, education, media entertainment

Understand Your Prospect's Industry

This is what I call home work and preparation to develop your personal sales plan. The more you know about your prospect, the more successful you become. I developed a questionnaire to guide you through this process of Understanding Your Prospect.

Select one of your three "expert" market sectors. Answer the questions in the following chart. If you don't have the answer for each question, just move on to the next one until you go through the entire questionnaire. Put a question mark (?) wherever you do not know the answer. This question mark (?) serves as a reminder for you to conduct the necessary research required to build your "Expert" Industry & Vertical Sector Profile.

Helpful Hint to do this assignment: Place the name of an existing client on the form and think about them as you answer the following questions.

Understand Your Prospect	Knowledge
1. Who are your existing clients in this sector? (List one or two existing clients who fit this major vertical.).	
2. How does the industry position your prospect in their industry? A champion and leader in technological solutions to gain competitive advantage?	
3. Where are they located? (Where is their head office? Where is the decision maker located? Locally? Overseas?)	
4. Where do they shop? (Locally, overseas, Internet?) Do they have an official buying process? (RFP is a mandatory practice if your vertical is government.)	

5. What is their buying behaviour? How do they buy? (Phone, Internet, distribution, retail electronic stores, in person?)	
6. What do they buy? (Hardware, software, appliances or a total integrated solution? What are considered commodity items? What are the specialty items?)	
7. What do they need? (What are the accelerator ingredients that keep their businesses thriving? What can they not live without? Do they buy a total solution package or are they a DIY shop?)	
8. What are their business challenges? What are the issues that keep them awake at night? What are their current IT challenges? (Challenges specific to this "major" target market.)	
9. What is their strategic plan and roadmap to maintain a competitive advantage in their industry? (What do they have planned for the future?)	
10. What is their budget range? Do they usually purchase based on new projects? If so, do they have a project budget?	
11. When do they expect delivery? (Same day, next day, 7 days? When is their busy season? Their slow season?)	
12. What is changing in their life? (Did the government change regulation on their industry? Such as dumpage fee, softwood lumber treaty, union labor dispute?)	
13. What would consistently make them feel special? (Only answer this question if you have asked them.)	

Do You Really Understand Your Client?

Were you able to answer all of the questions? Did you discover that you don't know as much about your clients as you thought?

Now you know why market research companies exist. They will find out all of this data for a reasonable fee. However, some of the data may not be current as the market condition changes. What concerns you is the accuracy of the information. The best and most reliable information is your own. You must develop and conduct your own target market research surveys by using the "Expert" Industry & Vertical Sector Profile. You update that prospect's profile every single time you have a meeting, make a phone call or interact with them.

Helpful Hint: *The objective is to anticipate your clients' needs and to exceed them. Use this Work Tool for ongoing reviews in your professional practice so you are current with business issues with your prospect.*

Finding High Quality Prospects

Now that you know what you are looking for, where do you find high quality prospects? Where to find your prospects in the target market that you have industry expertise in?

Association Membership Directory & Commercial Listings

Industry association memberships, publication subscriptions, your company's own prospect list, purchased lists, all of these will do. You should proceed with caution when you consider purchasing these lists. Make sure the information is current. Focus on your own target market!

Any lists that are printed on paper are usually at least six months old. It takes a list acquisition company at least three to six months to acquire the data, publish it, sell it, and distribute it. Therefore, some lists range anywhere from 12 to 18 months old.

"Changing of guard" is quite common with the fast changing pace in some industries. Decision makers get promoted, transferred, or simply leave the company. This dynamic cycle occurs anywhere from zero to 18 months before you purchase your list. All of these have an impact on the list's accuracy. The information could be out-off-date for your sales activities. It helps to have the most current names of the decision makers and their titles in your database.

Calling high has always been a challenge for most salespeople. It is prudent to start from the top. Decision makers, presidents, CEOs and VPs may be the only people you wish to speak with initially. They give you guidance in approaching their team members who are responsible for IT solutions. If you are a consultant for instance, operation managers are your internal competition. They are paid to know what you know. However, their boss, being the VP or president, usually sees the value of an impartial outsider who may reiterate exactly what their manager has been saying all along.

In summary, when using a list acquisition service, make sure that they are reputable and guarantee the quality of the data. They should also work with you in a consultative manner to help clearly determine the parameters of your Pipeline.

Helpful Hint: *Aim High! There is nothing more powerful than having the CEO or president— the top decision maker— refer you to the person who is in charge of the acquisition of your solutions.*

Newspapers

Newspapers! Either online or on paper, are another great place to find high quality prospects. Don't forget to look in the classified section. Companies that are growing or expanding are hiring. Spend some time browsing through career opportunities in you local major newspaper. You will find hiring ads that are IT oriented, including pre-implementation hints and post installation support.

If you are in the service industry, you will have noticed that more and more companies are embracing the concept of outsourcing, i.e. not hiring from within but actually contracting externally. Senior decision makers decide on cost-saving measures.

The business section of national newspapers is another place to find companies that are making changes. It reveals who the most recent decision makers are. Traditionally these are the leaders in the community. Senior Executive appointment notices are posted in the business section in major newspapers such as News USA, Globe and Mail, the Financial Post, Financial Times (GB), Wall Street Journal. These executive announcements give you the most up to date information on newly minted decision makers. You can be assured that the information should be 30 days old.

Consider subscribing to smaller local newspapers. These are a fabulous resource for high quality prospects. Within the pages is up-to-date information on the movers and shakers in that particular business community and their influencers.

Internet - Online Searches

Get connected on the web every day with your preferred local, national and international news service. Use Google to search for announcements in your target market.

Tips: *If your location is confined to the city limit, why not use the local newspaper's website as your default "Home" page. It will save you time. Also consider using their free email notification services. You will get notified when your searching criteria are met.*

Helpful Hint: *When researching your targeted prospect on the Internet, read the press releases before you read anything else. Find out who the players are and what is happening or projected to happen within that company.*

Referrals from Current Customers

Where is the best place to find high quality prospects? Start with your current customers.

Your clients should be referring business to you on an on-going basis. This is why it is extremely important to have a clearly defined Pipeline Parameter Statement. When your clients understand whom you help, they are more willing to introduce you to friends and colleagues who fit your description.

And, of course, do not forget to ask for referrals from clients who are not currently giving them to you. Make this exercise as a proactive activity and not "by chance" or "whenever you have time" attitude. It pays dividends in the long run. Just remember, you must earn the right!

Referrals Through Networking

www.Linkedin.com, www.plaxo.com are two popular professional networking sites. You can leverage your current business contacts and nurture the network to grow your business.

Start Your own BLOG & Professional Networking

Create your own network. Offering professional services to your network will help you generate more contacts.

Promote through webminars, executive briefings

Cost of traveling is escalating. Most executives are not traveling to conferences or tradeshows as often as they wish. You can generate interests through technology. Bring your presentation to their desktop.

Part II - The Buying Process

Understanding the Buying Process
Introduction

In the high tech industry, we have clearly defined the Buying Cycle of new technology and paradigm shifts. Stages of Buying Cycle of technology solutions are well acknowledged in the industry. The "early adopters", "crossing the chasm strategies", "mainstream", and "laggard categories" are well-accepted as stages of adoption in the high technology market. As sales professionals in the high tech industry, it is prudent that you keep the Technology Adoption Life Cycle model in mind when you speak to your prospect. This model maps very well with the Stages of Buying Cycle.

For example, let's examine the adoption of the automatic teller machine (ATM) by consumers. There are still people who prefer to wait in a bank line on a hard concrete floor until a teller can serve them. They don't want to change. They don't believe they need these ATMs. They may be a little defensive when the subject is broached. They may be completely in denial about the prospect of having to change their behaviour in the future. These folks are at Stage 1 *(Indifferent)* in the buying cycle when it comes to the utilization of an ATM. In the Technology Adoption Life Cycle, they are considered the laggards.

Another example is online banking services via the Internet. People accept this new convenient mode of banking transaction after a period of uncertainty, security assurance and finally ease of use. The early adopters took the new technology in stride while the mainstream consumers followed suit after they became comfortable with this online banking model.

A client (end user) at Stage 4 – *Committed*, who has not set foot in a bank for more than a year, conducts all of his or her banking through PC or telephone. He thinks it's the greatest convenient tool in the world. He has become an advocate of the concept and tells all of his friends and neighbors that this is the only way to bank.

Do you think you can get someone from Stage 1 (*Indifferent*) who is defensive, and uninterested to Stage 4 (*Committed*), which is total advocacy, in one interaction?

If you said "No!" you're right! You would realize soon that it takes anywhere from five to multiple "touches" (such as a networking function, a meeting, a phone call, a brochure, a video clip, an email, a testimonial, reference letter, an invoice) before anyone will completely embrace a new idea and a new technology solution. Accelerating the selling process can mean reducing the number of touches. How to utilize technologies to facilitate these necessary "touches" will produce results efficiently!

You will discover that when you meet people in our marketing, sales or client service world, they fit within one of the *Stages of Buying Cycle*. They could be an advocate, a client or, as you found in the first learning module *The Pipeline – Target Your Market*, a "prospect."

Each Stage of the Buying Cycle relates to people with whom you are doing business. By facilitating the buying process, you will be 100% focused on the prospect and existing client! Generally speaking, people buy because they have a problem they wish to solve. The perceived problems your prospect experiences become your "opportunities."

It is your responsibility to clearly identify the level of Buying Cycle of your prospect, client or advocate with respect to actively solving their particular problem in that moment of time. Then, it is your duty to help them move forward. When you acquire the expertise and skills in identification and understanding of their business problems, you accelerate the sales process with results. The next most important skill is to solve these business problems with your technology offerings.

Classifying Stages of Buyer's Buying Cycle

It is important to identify the exact Stage of Buying Cycle of your prospect within first 15 minutes of your first fact finding meeting, or at the end of the meeting. This meeting may be conducted either over the phone or face-to-face. After you have classified them accurately, you can organize your resources to build a meaningful relationship with them.

The Stage of Buying Cycle will determine how you will treat them. As you will see, a Stage 1 prospect has a completely different "mindset" than one at Stage 4.

You have a quantifiable method to determine exactly where your prospects are in their Stage of the buying process. You cannot afford to misjudge the current Stage of Buying Cycle of a prospect. Do not assume or guess their level of interest. Subjective guessing is usually wrong. Do it scientifically using the Qualification ScoreCard in Part III. By accurately accessing their Stage in the buying cycle, you save time and resources. As you will see in Part III, the next module, *Qualifying Process – Assign the Stage of Buying Cycle,* this systematic process will accurately categorize your prospect in an objective, measurable scorecard.

Classifying the Stages of Buying Cycle will help you to:

▶ Prioritize your activities,

▶ Determine with whom you should spend your time, and more importantly, inspire them to buy from you.

When qualifying your prospects, you must first relate the Stage of Buying Cycle to the person with whom you are dealing.

Let's explore the Stages of Buying Cycle in general terms.

Stages of Buyers' Buying Cycle are:

1. Indifferent
2. Interested
3. Qualified
4. Committed
5. Closed (Sold)

Speed of Change

How can you accelerate the selling process from Stage 1 Indifferent to Stage 5 Closed?

First, recognize the current Stage of Buying Cycle of your prospects when you first meet them. Most of the time, your prospects do not come to you at *Stage 1 - Indifferent*. They arrive on your radar at different s of their buying cycle. You must be alert and start your qualifying process immediately. Categorize them at the appropriate stage of the buying cycle so you can organize your team. Plan your sales activities accordingly.

The length of time required to move the prospect from one stage to the next varies from project to project. There is no set duration of time that your prospect must remain at every stage of the buying cycle. Time can be expressed in units of time in seconds, minutes, hours, days, weeks or months. The amount of time generally is directly proportional to the size, complexity and financial investment level of your solution. If you sell electronic medical record systems to the Ministry of Health in California, your unit of measurement for time will be in months or even years. You have to establish your own benchmark to estimate how long a prospect is likely to remain in one particular Stage of Buying Cycle. This dwelling time will also impact accuracy in your sales forecast report. Selling complex expensive enterprise systems involves a long sales cycle.

Timing is Everything

Logically, the unit measurement of time is proportional to the potential revenues to be generated from the deal.
For example, a multi-million dollar electronic medical record development project will take many, many months to close. It may take anywhere from 6 to 24 months to inspire a decision maker from Stage 1 to Stage 5.

Another example, a government agency, a Stage 3 – Qualified prospect, may require six months or longer to complete all bureaucratic paperwork and processes, even though they are qualified to do business with you.

Stage of Buying Cycle is a dynamic state of mind exhibited by your prospect. You must be alert to this constant change of behaviour of your prospect. They do not remain in one particular Stage. They change their perspectives during their journey through the buying cycle.

Your company experience with your clients' behaviour during the 12 months will provide an accurate benchmark to gauge the average time needed to close a deal. It is important that you keep track of the time and resources and log their behaviour over time. Your objective is to inspire your prospect to change his behaviour through every stage of the buying cycle to the ultimate Stage of *Closed/Sold*.

Stage 1 - Indifferent

Definition: Your prospect has no intention of trying something new at this moment in time.

Indicators: Your prospect is:

▶ Not aware of any long term consequences of his behaviour

▶ Not interested in thinking about the problem, may be in denial

▶ Often defensive in response to any pressure to accept a new idea or concept

▶ Often demoralized about their inability to change

From your *Pipeline,* you have identified a prospect with whom you have carefully chosen to develop a relationship. Counting on the premise that "change is constant," you know that if he does not have a problem now, he will have one eventually. Using this simple methodology, you will be there to assist them.

Stage 1 *Indifferent* prospect is probably not interested in speaking with you. He does not know what is available to him, or he is in self-denial state. He is unaware of the benefits of new technology available on the market. He might have just bought from someone else, or is very happy with his or her current vendor.

Generally, at Stage 1, it is assumed that six months is as far into the future as people will anticipate making a specific behavioral change.

Assignment*: Write the names of two prospects that fit the description of Stage 1 – Indifferent.*

_____

_____

_____

Stage 2 - Interested

Definition: Your prospect recognizes the problem and starts researching.

Indicators: Your prospect is:

▶ Actively engaged in information seeking activities and gathering information for their next steps. (For example, White Papers in related subjects, Case Studies from your company or reputable third party sources would be downloaded by this group of prospects.)

▶ Beginning to re-evaluate themselves in light of the possibility of doing things differently (What if scenario analysis! Evaluate the alternates.)

▶ Talking and listening and open to testimonials, best practices and references

▶ Assessing the pros and cons of alternate offerings

Responses from these prospects include, "Really? And what else does your product do?" Or, "How would you see that working for us?" They are surfing the net, checking out your website and that of your competitors, gathering brochures and collecting data. They are beginning to form the intent to act, but they do not have a deadline in mind. They may have one to six plus months in their time frame to move forward.

Warning! *They could remain at this stage indefinitely! They've been collecting information for months; sometimes years and never seem to be able to make a commitment. These are the ones you have to watch out for, not the Stage 1 Indifferent prospects. They are potential time wasters.*

Assignment: *Write two names of prospects that fit this description.*

_____

_____

_____

_____

_____

Stage 3 - Qualified

Definition: Your prospect intends to take action in the near future.

Indicators: Your prospect has:

▶ Developed a plan of action

▶ Set up a steering committee including all stakeholders

▶ Organized a project team with well defined roles and functions

▶ Set goals and established a timeline

▶ Been gathering more definitive information

▶ Most importantly funding approved/to be confirmed

When companies have issued a Request for Proposal (RFP), they are not necessarily, in Stage 3 - *Qualified*.   It depends on whether they have a definitive deadline for the project.

You have several questions to ponder upon:

▶ "What is their 'critical deadline?"

▶ "Does the acquisition of a new product or service depend upon meeting a certain deadline?"

▶ "Does it fit our time frame?"

If you answer "No" or "None" to these questions, they are not your Stage 3 *Qualified* prospects.

This is the reason why you are now seeing more "Requests for Information" (RFI) instead of RFP (Request for Proposal). Receipt of an RFI can be an indication that you are dealing with a prospect at Stage 2 - *Interested* instead of a Stage 3 - *Qualifier*. It is to your advantage when you are involved at the RFI Stage. You have the time to work with your prospect before the official issuance of an RFP. Help your prospect to define the criteria of the solution. It helps you to increase your probability of winning. However, if you missed the "input" phase to the RFI, your chance of winning RFP later is uncertain.

You must pick a fight when you have a chance of winning. A sure win is preferable than a fight in an open battlefield.

RFP = Request for Proposal

RFI = Request for Information

Heads up! *Prospects **at** Stage 3 Qualified, want to change. They are in a transitional Stage and want to make change quickly. So, don't lose out on your very narrow "Window of Opportunity".*

Assignment: *Write two names of prospects that fit this description.*

Stage 4 - Committed

Definition: Your prospect is actively engaged in problem solving.

Indicators: Your prospect:

▶ Is appointing personnel to tasks

▶ Has assigned a budget (i.e. has allocated project funding)

▶ Is busier than all the other Stages?

▶ Is funding allocation confirmed and approved?

Warning!   *Of all the Stages, Stage 4 - Committed is the most susceptible to slipping back. **This is the most vulnerable period of your selling cycle. Your competitors are in action. Your prospect is committed. You blink, you lose.***

The deal is not done until the money is in the bank. When you thought that you just finished making the deal of the century, you rushed back to the office completely elated. You're telling everyone, "I got the deal!" You're ringing bells, shaking hands, giving high-fives all around until someone asks, "Yes, congratulations. But did you get the cheque?" You look at them blankly and say, "No, but the deal is in the bag. Don't worry, I'll get the cheque." And then, a week goes by, no cheque. Another week goes by and your prospect does not return your calls. Finally, weeks go by and your prospect has stopped responding to your emails and requests for appointments.

What happened to your order? Your prospect slipped back, all the way from Stage 4 to Stage 3 to 2 to Stage 1. Why? They either bought from someone else or made a decision to delay the purchase. People can move up and down the Stages of Buying Cycle during the buying process. How do you prevent this from happening? Get that Purchase Order and finish the paper work.

Assignment: *Write two names of prospects that fit this description.*

_____

_____

_____

_____

_____

_____

Stage 5 - Closed/Sold

Definition: Deal is done. It is also the beginning of a new relationship.

Indicators: ☒ There is a signed contract.

        ☒ 100% of the payment has been received.

        ▶ Specific expectations have been clearly outlined.

        ▶ Your client is relying heavily upon you to remind them of why they invested in the first place.

Heads Up! *Beware of "buyers' remorse!" Our Stage 5 Closed/Sold client has plenty of people in their organization asking to remind them of the benefits of their decision.*

Closed prospects need to have their decision continually validated until the symptom of "buyer's remorse" is removed. You must reassure your prospects that their decision was a wise one, and to continue to remind them for as long as it takes. They need reinforcement from your company that you want them as a Lifelong Customer. It is a subtle, hidden behaviour. Be proactive to follow through with this activity.

You want to continually meet and surpass their expectations so they will:

▶ Continue to purchase from you and no one else

▶ Want to buy new products from you.

▶ Refer business to you on a regular basis

▶ Be 100% loyal for at least six months?

Helpful Hint: *Ensure that your final proposals serve as your contractual agreement. It must specifically outline exactly what the client's* *expectations are in order for you to fulfill the contract. This should also stipulate what you require from them to guarantee successful delivery of your solution.*

Assignment: *Write two names of prospects that fit this description.*

1.

2.

What percentage of Stage 5 **Closed** Prospect will become lifelong customers and you do not need to ever make another cold call again?

A loyal Lifelong Customer will continue to do business with you. You have special privileges now because you have credibility and a proven track record with them. Your business volume will grow based on the trusting relationship. You are now in an enviable position, as your company did not even invest in advertising funding; rather you must maintain superior customer service. You have earned your respect and you should ask for referrals from this loyal customer. You finally become their trusted advisor. Please note that this is the ultimate goal of every salesperson during their sales career.

How Do You Scientifically Quantify?

You must notice that the definitions of each Stage of Buying Cycle are somewhat arbitrary and subjective. They are open to interpretation. You know that the prospect arrives on your radar screen at different Stages. He has his own set of perceived problems. Your goal is to qualify your prospect scientifically to determine his Stage of Buying Cycle.

This is a binary action. There is no "gray area" when it comes to classifying your prospects. You must be able to objectively determine exactly which Stage of the Buying Cycle your prospects are in, at that particular moment, in highly quantifiable terms. It should not be a subjective judgment call on your part.

You learned that a Stage 1 **Indifferent** prospect can be defensive and hostile because he does not want to deal with his problem at that moment. There is a possibility that he is not aware of new technological solutions. Nonetheless, with polite probing, you can find out more about his state of mind.   Please do not pre-judge his stage in the Buying Cycle.

Through the *Qualifying* process – *Assign the Stage of Buying Cycle*, you learn how to accurately assess the opportunities presented to you.

Part III – Qualification Process

Qualification Process

Introduction

In the Stages of Buying Cycle module, you will discover five types of prospects and two types of clients.

Prospects are classified as

1. Indifferent
2. Interested
3. Qualified
4. Committed
5. Closed (Sold)

Clients (Customers) are classified as SOLD and Lifelong Customer.

Keys to Qualifying

Now that you have learnt the definitions and indicators of each Stage of Buying Cycle, let's examine the scientific method that you can use to accurately qualify prospects within the first 15 minutes. Your objective is to get them through the Pipeline by engaging with your prospects proactively. Assign them a Stage of Buying Cycle immediately upon your first encounter. This is the baseline that you start working from. Qualifying is the act of assigning your prospects a Stage of Buying Cycle at that particular moment.

You will learn about two tools to effectively complete this important task: the *Qualification Questionnaire* and the *Qualification Scorecard*.

Using these tools is like taking a "snapshot" of an opportunity with your prospects. While the *Qualification Scorecard becomes* your camera, the Qualification Questionnaire is the instant digital picture of the opportunity. To effectively manage your opportunity to increase your revenues, you must accurately observe and track the changes demonstrated by your prospects.

Use your **Qualification Questionnaire** and **Qualification Scorecard** each and every time you engage with your prospects. Their Stage of Buying Cycle will change until they reach Stage 5 – *Closed/ Sold*. For example, one moment they may think that you are the greatest advisor in his world and next, they are not providing you with any more business. There is no "pre-qualifying step", except your own research and knowledge of the particular prospect. You must continually <u>re-qualify</u> them, each and every time you communicate with them.

The accuracy of your **Qualification Questionnaire** and its companion **Qualification Scorecard** depends upon the accuracy of your analysis of the current situation into a binary (Yes/No) assessment.

Snapshot - Health Check

To accurately assess your prospect's Stage in the buying cycle; you need information in only four areas of their business.

Qualification	Question for Ourselves
Product & Service Alignment	1. Does the prospect perceive a fit with us?
People	2. Who are the Decision Makers and Influencers and what is the decision making process?
Time Frame	3. Is there a "critical deadline" and can we meet it?
Budget Funding	4. Are funds currently allocated for this project?

Helpful Hint: *To accurately complete your Scorecard you must answer each of these questions with a definitive "Yes" or "No."*

Qualification Scorecard

Date: _____

Name of the Opportunity: _____

Potential Revenue: _____ Fiscal Year End: _____

CRITERIA	Y/N	Y/N	Y/N
Product Alignment ((Solution for business Pain)			
People (Decision Maker(s))			
Time Line/Milestone Critical Deadline Date: _____			
Budget Funding Allocated _____ $			
STAGE OF BUYING CYCLE			
STAGE OF OPPORTUNITY			

It is important to design a well-developed *Qualification Questionnaire* to uncover the answers to these four major criteria of qualification. This usually comprises of at least five questions in each criteria for a total of 20 questions. With this worksheet, you can select the appropriate questions to uncover critical data. Place a quantifiable "Y" (Yes) or "N" (No) in each of the relevant boxes on your *Qualification Scorecard*.

Remember, you might have approximately 15 minutes in your meeting to obtain sufficient data to update your Qualification Scorecard. If you have the luxury of ample time at your fact-finding meeting, take advantage of the privilege of time set aside by your prospect. Encourage your prospects to talk about themselves and their perceived business pain as much as possible.

Why do you need five different ways to ask each question? One motivator in human behaviour is fear. However, self-preservation is considered as a strong motivator in business. Business people always make sure that they don't look bad in front of their peers, mates, bosses, co-workers, or any affiliates.

In the interest of self-preservation, your prospect may respond to your fact finding questions with an exaggeration of the truth. From your experience, how many times have you asked the question, "Who was in charge of the purchase?" and your prospect said, "Me." Later in the buying cycle, you uncover that he was not actually responsible for the purchase; rather his boss is the decision maker. You didn't find out until it was too late in the buying cycle. He is actually the gatekeeper who prevents you from reaching the true decision maker at an early stage of the buying cycle.

It is important to design your own *Qualification Questionnaire* for your business sector and "expert" industry sector. If you require guidance to develop your customized *Qualification Questionnaire*, discuss it with your coach or seek assistance from an expert. (See *The Pipeline - Your Target Market* module.) A smart prospect will recognize your value from the professional questions you ask. You show your care and due diligence to learn more about him and his business. You fundamentally differentiate your professionalism from that of your competition.

Sounds pretty simple, doesn't it? Well, it is! A carefully prepared *Qualification Questionnaire* will enable you to obtain valuable information about the opportunity presented within the first five to 15 minutes. Let's continue to learn how to build the *Qualification Questionnaire*.

Refining Your Questioning (Dialogue) Skills

How do you inspire your prospect to feel safe when sharing with you their corporate information? Simply focus on the following fundamentals:

1. Establish rapport
2. Cite commonality
3. State clearly "What is in it for them"
4. Use open-ended questions to explore business pains

Closed-ended questions provide you with a "Yes" or "No" answer. They do not deliver any informative data. Closed-ended questions trap you into a corner and do not offer your prospect any airtime to expand his opinions or feelings or perception of his business pains or challenges. To avoid this, you must use open-ended questions that start with:

▶ How
▶ What
▶ Where
▶ Who
▶ When

To avoid potential irritation to your prospect, do not start with "WHY." "WHY" questions create an atmosphere of defensiveness. How do you feel when someone asked you a "WHY" question? You feel defensive and challenged. Your prospect would be placed in an awkward situation when you ask a "Why" question about his business operation. You can still ask the "why" question diplomatically without offending your prospect. You will learn how to do that as you refine your questioning skills later in this WorkBook.

Helpful Hint: *When you are stuck or wish to drill down on a point a little more, simply ask, "Would you enlighten me on...?" You will be surprised by the results. From now on, replace the word "Why" in your vocabulary, at home and at work, with more positive questions. Try it with no question mark inflection at the end and witness the reduction of stress in your life.*

Other Questioning Skill Suggestions

Begin your questions with a preemptive statement,

> ▶ "Help me understand... "
> ▶ "Out of curiosity..."
> ▶ "Tell me more about..."
> ▶ "Could you elaborate..."

You can always preempt your questions with a situation comment...

> ▶ "With the current financial crunch in the market, what are the impacts on your expansion program?"

Helpful Hint: *At the beginning of the conversation determine how much time they have to speak with you. Then divide the time up into **four parts** to ensure that you have enough time to accurately assess the data in each criteria quadrant on your Scorecard.*

More suggestions:

> ▶ Speak only 25% of the time
> ▶ Do not give out too much information and start selling
> ▶ Overcome objections (including perceived ones too)
> ▶ Complete all four boxes on your Qualification ScoreCard
> ▶ Upon completion, schedule next steps

Warning! *Questions that start with "Do", "Don't" or "Should" may yield the same results as speaking the word "Why." Avoid using these words at all times.*

Preparation

Needless to say, do your homework. When you include a prospect in your Pipeline, you should have some basic knowledge about their company and their industry. With diligent preparation prior to your first fact finding meeting, you should have a basic level of understanding of this prospect. What may be missing are your prospect's individual needs and his perceived business problems.

Preparation is the utmost important step to demonstrate your professionalism before your walk into the first meeting with your prospect. Pay attention to current news, announcements, recent government regulation, any merger/acquisitions, and their challenges due to economic conditions. You MUST prepare a list of fact finding questions for your interviews. Bring your ears and listen attentively. If you are making a joint call with your manager, you must brief him prior to the meeting with the prospect. Some companies have an unwritten rule about "briefing in writing" for any joint sales calls with their superior. In this executive briefing, you must outline the objective of the meeting and confirm the time made available to you by your prospect.

There are many areas that you can research for your preparation. Let's examine these facilities that are available to you at no cost and available at your fingertips.

Library: You can find files of newspaper clippings, announcements of executive appointments, annual reports, and relevant industry articles about the company in libraries.

Your Own Internal Resources: Your own marketing department may already have information on this prospect on file. Check with your support team. Quite frequently, you find lots of valuable information by Googling it in your Intranet. Seek help from your channel partners, strategic alliances and your internal business divisions.

Internet: Use the Internet to your advantage. This is a convenient starting point. Your prospect's website is the obvious source for basic information such as the nature and size of their business. You may find a BLOG under the company's website. You will find product information, executive profiles, and their board of directors on their website. It may even reveal their current focus or challenges.

Find out what changes have transpired in their operation and industry. How these changes have affected their business and industry? When you make that first contact, you will impress your prospect immensely if you already have a preliminary concept of what their challenges are. Your efforts to become their trusted advisor will be well served when you build a deep understanding of your prospect's world.

Here is a checklist to ensure that you have completed your preparations, before you engage in communication with your prospect:

Preparation Research Checklist

▶ What is their website address?

▶ What do the newswire and financial credit services say? How do their financials compare to similar companies?

▶ What is their business? What are their revenue and profit trends? What's changing?

▶ What are their products and services?

▶ What are their key markets? Who are their key clients?

▶ Who are their key competitors?

▶ What are their industry challenges? Are they growing or shrinking?

Tip: *When researching on the Internet, where do you begin? Our suggestion is to read their press releases first. Then check out the other news services online. Don't forget about utilizing the credit services that you can subscribe to online. Remember, one of your Pipeline Parameters is "credit worthiness"*

Now you are ready to start developing questions that will help you to accurately assign a Stage of Buying Cycle for your prospect.

Aligning "Problems" with "Solutions" (The Match)

Does the prospect perceive a fit with your company's product and services?

People buy to either resolve a problem or make a change. To determine where they are in their buying Stage, you must first understand their business pain. You will determine if there is a perceived match between their needs and your offerings. You arrive at such a conclusion by asking a few carefully crafted questions early in your sales campaign. When you determine that there is no fit at this time, stop at this qualifying phase. On your Scorecard, you assign them to Stage 1 - *Indifferent*. You can then either pleasantly refer them to your friendly competitor or place them in your nurturing campaign. Then, move on to the next prospect in your Pipeline.

To properly rule-out this prospect, you must ask yourself another qualifying question. "What is their perspective on my expertise? Do they consider me or my company as the trusted advisor?" Is there any future business potential with this prospect? Is this a strategic prospect to have in my portfolio to help in building my business? When you are satisfied with the answers to these questions, you place a quantifiable "Yes" or "No" in this qualification section of your Scorecard.

Another important factor is to evaluate their loyalty to other suppliers, especially your competitors. It is important to know early in your sales campaign if they had made a heavy investment in staff training on your competitor's technology. If they invested thousands of dollars to educate their IT staff on Microsoft Exchange, you will have an uphill battle to dismantle such an infrastructure. Your Open Mail system does not have a chance to succeed in this company. However, under very unusual circumstances, you may have a chance if your prospect is experiencing extreme intolerable technical problems at this very moment.

Assignment: *Take a few moments to write down five questions to help understand their need and ensure that it matches what your company provides. Develop questions to uncover: (1) Who is the dominant IT supplier* *for this prospect? (2) How happy are they with this competitor of yours? (3) What do they buy from them? For how long have they been purchasing from them?*

_____

_____

_____

_____

The Players

Who are the decision makers and influencers and what is their internal decision making process?

Three types of "players" are decision makers, influencers, and end users. They disguise themselves in an array of titles. However, their true authority may be hidden behind their titles. You must know with whom the decision making authority resides. You must uncover who they are, who influences that decision and who ultimately makes the decision. Some purchasing decisions are made by consensus. Presidents and CEOs rely on informed decisions made by the people around them including the Board of Directors and outside consultants.

Having an in-depth knowledge of their decision making process is important. During this learning process, you will identify the roles and authorities of all the players. Roles of these players are in dynamic state. They will change depending on the premise of the company and the industry environment. Create one box for each player on your Scorecard. The list of Decision Makers can expand over time. At one point, a client of mine had 18 names, positions and responsibilities identified on their Scorecard by the time the deal was done.

Tips: *Things to consider while you develop questions for your Interaction Questionnaire:*

Identify the key decision makers and their circle of influence. Who are the other stakeholders for this project? Continue to update your *Questionnaire* and *ScoreCard* every time you communicate with the players so that you compare actual against perceived "authority" of these individuals.

Do they work with any third party consulting firms? Who are their external trusted advisors? Do they outsource their operation to an outside third party? Or do they use selective outsourced individuals for special projects due to lack of internal expertise?

Assignment: *Write down the titles of all the possible Decision Makers and Influencers who could be involved during your revenue building process and their respective responsibilities.*

Title	Responsibilities
Outside Consultant	Advisor to the President, Sales Coach
VP Operation Plant	Human resources for plant workers, shipping and receiving, operation of equipment and manufacturing.

Heads up! *To place a quantifiable "Y" or "N" in your Qualification Scorecard, the ultimate question to ask is, "Does this Player have the authority to sign off on the investment for our solution?"*

Qualifying the Players

What questions are appropriate to ask "Who are the Decision Makers and Influencers and what is your decision making process?"

Assignment: *Take a few moments to write down five questions using your refined interviewing skills to uncover the possible Influencers and Decision Makers.*

Right from the start, it is important to demonstrate with your prospect that your relationship is based upon mutual collaboration. To facilitate the interview process, we suggest that you first state, "As your partner on this project, it is really important that you are involved with all of the Decision Makers..."

Example: Whom outside of your organization do you like to involve in the decision-making process?

_____

_____

_____

_____

_____

_____

TimeLine (Milestone)

Is there a critical deadline and can you deliver to meet the deadline?

To place a "Yes" or "No" in the Time Frame (TimeLine) quadrant, it is imperative that you understand the amount of time required to successfully close the deal.

There are many sales activities to perform to inspire Stage 4 – *Committed Prospects* to move to Stage 5 - *Closed/Sold*. Consider the length of time required to develop a proposal. You must also know the amount of time you need to conduct an assessment study to present to all decision makers. If you have to complete a diagnostic, to arrange a presentation of the proposal, to negotiate the contract, and to arrange for post sales support and product delivery, you should estimate the length of time to manage all the necessary activities and steps. It's crucial to be realistic and examine the possibility of completing the deal.

Milestones on the Road

Milestones are events that are usually tied to a date or a period. For instance, a manufacturing company might have to wait for testing or specification approval before they negotiate with their component suppliers. You must be alert to other uncontrollable macro economic factors, government fiscal and monetary policy, and industry trends that may impact your prospect during their buying cycle.

Assignment: Using the chart below, list all of the tasks that you and your prospect must complete to close a significantly large deal. Include everything from the outbound business development call to signing the contracts. Then list the time range required to complete each task. At the bottom, add up the time range required to close a deal.

Events/Milestones	Time Range to Complete
Example: Independent laboratory testing	Example: 3 to 5 weeks
Total:	_____ to _____ weeks/months

The Road to Success

Now plot these tasks on an Execution Milestone TimeLine.

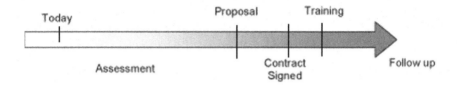

There are many factors that impact their readiness for adopting a transition technology plan or a complete make over deployment. For example, what is their fiscal year end? What do they do with the excess budget funding at the end of their fiscal year? How about their current IT infrastructure: What kind of network do they have? What is the server architecture? Standard of the company IT supplier (are they an HP, IBM, Cisco shop?

How long does it take to close the deal from the time you conduct your _Needs Assessment_ to signing the contract? Is it three weeks? Is it six months? Or longer depending on the scope of the opportunity? Does this match the date by which the prospect requires their solution? Do you have enough time? When you demonstrate your ability to take care of these finer details early in the game, you earn the respect of your prospect. You strengthen your relationship with your prospect. Use this worksheet to help you to establish the length of time that you require to successfully close the deal.

Window of Opportunity (Window of Activities)

Window of Opportunity is defined as, "A short period of time during which an opportunity must be acted on or missed".

Identifying your prospect's Window of Opportunity requires careful construction of your questions. You must understand your prospect's business timelines and synchronize them with yours.

Establishing these milestones will assist you in this activity. Some salespeople don't have a clear idea of _when_ the prospect needs to make a change. Quite often, it is because the prospect is in the early Stages of their buying cycle and he has no looming deadline. Sometimes, the salesperson simply hasn't asked the right question about the time line. Do not guess their time line. Sometimes, your prospect may have no control about the time line. Just ask the question and expect a response from the prospect.

Knowing their time line early gives you the space to plan. You can gauge your sale activities according to your prospect's plan of action. He has to make a decision about who to select as their provider and their deadline of deployment. It is your professional responsibility to inspire him to change and to improve the business operation. You should collaborate to define the roadmap with him, an action to achieve their goals. These dates will affect your "Window of Opportunity."

Helpful Hint: *As a professional solution provider, it is imperative that legal agreements are signed and sealed in time to assure that the "critical deadline" is not missed.*

Time Frame

Timeline information gives you a schedule to plan your sales activities, to move your prospect forward through the stages of their buying cycle.

Assignment: *Take a few moments to write down the questions that will uncover the milestones, critical deadline and Window of Opportunity using the captioned road to success.*

Helpful Hint: *Ask," When is your fiscal year end?" It provides the perfect "bridge" between Time Frame and Allocation of Funds.*

Example: What outside influences could affect your schedule for implementation?

_____

_____

_____

_____

_____

_____

_____

_____

_____

_____

Allocation of Funds
Are funds currently allocated for this project?

Most sales people have a difficult time talking about money in their first meeting with their prospect. It is considered as impolite in a social setting. In business however, it is considered professional, especially by senior business executives.

Your *Qualification Scorecard* is incomplete until the question; "Are funds currently allocated for this project?" is addressed. You should have several versions of the same question in your arsenal. This is very critical in your qualification process.

The question, "Is there a budget?" may not reveal if there is actual funding available. How many times have you asked this question only to find out that there were never any funds allocated even though there is a budget? "Budget" may imply work in progress but there are conditions attached to the "budget". The word "budget" may not reveal the true level of authority of this individual. Use caution with the word "budget" and the context that it is used in.

Helpful Hint: *Money can always be found when value is perceived. You need to know if the funds are available today and how long they are available.*

Assignment: *Develop as many euphemisms as you can to replace the word "budget" so you can use them in your question development.*

Example: Investment can be used in place of "budget".

_____

_____

_____

_____

_____

Allocation of Funds

__Assignment:__ Write down five Allocation of Funds questions using your "budget" euphemisms from the prior page. Don't forget to use open-ended questions. Find the best word or cluster of words that will quickly unveil the real situation

Example: What funds are currently allocated for this project?

_____

_____

_____

_____

_____

_____

_____

_____

_____

Thought triggering questions:

What do they do with the excess budget funding at the end of their fiscal year?

Which departments might the funding come from?

How do they like to buy? Do they prefer to finance or spend cash?

Develop Your Own Qualification Questionnaire

You should now have at least 20 questions for your _Qualification Questionnaire_.

Place an asterisk (*) next to your "killer" question in each quadrant that you feel is the most effective in uncovering high quality information. These will be the *four* questions to ask when you have less than five minutes to assess any opportunities. You can call this "_Elevator Assessment Questions_". You will find these _Elevator Assessment Questions_ very useful in a tradeshow environment, or a social networking event. The key is to internalize these four questions so you don't need to turn to your Qualification Scorecard.

The Scientific Method

The accuracy of your Qualification Questionnaire and its companion Qualification Scorecard depends upon three things:

▶ Clarity of your questions

▶ Your understanding of their situation

▶ Accuracy of your analysis into a binary (Yes/No) assessment

Information gathered and interpreted at that specific moment are strictly snapshots of your prospect's status. It is your understanding of their current business at that moment. That is why it is important to always utilize these tools each and every time you communicate with your prospects.

Review the following for an example of a Qualification Questionnaire tool used by a client in the CRM software industry. You can use this example as the base model to develop your own Questionnaire.

Developing Your Own Qualification Questionniare

Product Alignment - Is there a match between your service and your prospect's business pain? Does your prospect perceive a fit?

1. What do you wish to accomplish?
2. What are the most important functions that you require?
3. How are these tasks handled now?
4. In addition to _____, what challenges are you facing in your industry?
5. When it comes to _____, what are the three key qualities that are most important to you?

Players - Who are all of the Decision Makers and Influencers, and what is their decision making process?

6. What is your role in this project?
7. Who else is involved in this project?
8. Who initiated this project?
9. What is your decision making process?
10. Who, other than yourself, needs to be involved in the decision making process?
11. Who will be involved in the implementation of your solution?
12. Which outside consultants are working on this project with you?
13. Which department is driving this project?

Time Line - What is the critical deadline?

14. When do you need to make this decision?
15. When do you plan to take action with regards to this project?
16. How long have you have been looking for a solution?
17. When would you like everything completed?

18. What is driving these dates?

19. What is your schedule for implementation? Is it documented?

20. What will happen if you don't make this change?

Budget Funding - Are funds currently allocated for this project?

21. When is your fiscal year end?

22. You mentioned that this project was being driven by the _____ department, how are they financially responsible for this project?

23. What is your budgeting process?

24. Currently, what funds have been allocated to this project? From which department?

25. Our solutions range anywhere from $_____ to $ _____. How does this fit your requirements?

Assigning Stage of Buying Cycle

The *Qualification Scorecard* is a dynamic measurement tool to reflect the buying-cycle stage of your prospect. Your prospect's business environment is constantly changing because of many factors, either controllable or uncontrollable. You can adopt the following matrix (Example) to accommodate your particular sale situation. If you have several decision makers, create extra "rows" for each of them. This *Scorecard* is a very efficient, simple tool that you can utilize for account planning with your team, your coach and your management team. Use it as an executive briefing template when you make joint calls with your superior. You can even expand the *Scorecard* as a pseudo forecast sheet for your management. Be creative and expand on it.

Use the following matrix as your guide when assigning your Stage of Buying Cycle for your prospect.

Qualification Scorecard Matrix (Example)

Date of Snapshot	07/12/2001	7/25/01	8/15/01	09/12/2001	10/12/2001
	(Y/N = 1/0)	(Y/N = 1/0)	(Y/N = 1/0)	(Y/N = 1/0)	(Y/N = 1/0)
Product Alignment (Match)	1	1	1	1	1
Players	0	0	1	0	1
Time Frame	0	1	1	1	1
Funds	0	0	0	1	1
Stage of Opp	1	2	3	3	4

Mathematically, this is a binary model that uses "1" for "Yes" and "0" for "No". When you use an Excel Worksheet, you will minimize any mathematical error.

Let's walk through this example one Quadrant at a time:

1. **Product Alignment Quadrant:** This is a key factor if you uncover a "No" regardless of what else you discover in any other quadrant. If it is not a fit, please leave the scene. A "No" in the Alignment Quadrant means there is absolutely no real or perceived *fit* for your solution at this time.

2. **Player Quadrant:** If you have a "No" next to Decision Maker, you have a Stage 1 Indifferent. If you do not know the answer to a question that you must answer in the Scorecard, place a question mark with the letter "N" in the box. This will indicate that you have some more work to do. If your prospect perceives a fit and he is a Decision Maker, he is at least a Stage 2 – *Interested prospect*. You have a live one.

3. **Time Frame Quadrant:** When your prospect has no looming deadline, you know they are at Stage 1 – *Indifferent* in their buying cycle. You know how to allocate your resources for this client. Do not do a proposal prematurely.

4. **Funding Quadrant:** When your prospect is still working on funding approval, you give them a "No". You follow the money in your revenue generation activity. When the prospect has no funding allocation for this opportunity, you should not forecast this opportunity to your boss. Since this is a binary model, your sale forecast for this is "zero".

Bottom Line to Use the ScoreCard: It is important to understand these qualifying critical Stages and recognize them early. Your prospect has different mindsets depending on his Stage of Buying Cycle and he exhibits different behaviors accordingly. You know that you are not dealing with different types of people; rather you are dealing with their level of acceptance.

Use the example above to create your own Scorecard for your individual prospects. You will be surprised at how much you don't know about your prospects and their opportunities. By now, you should have a more realistic perspective of your pipeline. This ScoreCard enables you to forecast more accurately. You will be more convincing when you solicit assistances from your internal team of resources, your manager, and your company.

Helpful Hint: *It is very important to go through this analysis step using your two new tools, the Qualification Scorecard and the Qualification Questionnaire, to fully understand the Five Stages of Buying Cycle. You will experience that communication will be productive, relationships will be strengthened and more lifelong customers will be created.*

Example of a Scorecard

Date: ___May 8, 2001___
Name of the Opportunity: ___Gatos Software Inc___
Potential Revenue: ___$320,000___ **Fiscal Year End:** _Feb 28_

Date	March 10	March 31	May 8
Product Alignment	1	1	1
Players (Decision Makers)	1	1	1
Time Frame Critical Deadline Date: _____	0	1	1
Funds Allocated _____ $	0	0	1
STAGE OF BUYING CYCLE	2	3	4

Analyzing the Opportunity

Heads up! *Never assume that the person who signs the cheque is the only Decision Maker on a project.*

It is not relevant to assume that the CEO has the ultimate signing authority though the CEO must sign off on major initiatives. Depending on the operation structure of your prospect company, the CEO may rely heavily on his VP to choose the solution. He is willing to provide funding when the time is right. The CEO, as the VP's boss, needs to rubber stamp the project as a matter of mandated protocol. Players carry different weights in the decision making process. You can assign a "weight" scale to the players in your sale environment for your prospects. The total score for Players must be "1" to provide consistency in your scientific grading model. Use your judgment so you maintain consistency in the accuracy of your *Scorecard*.

Using Your Qualification Tools

Reflect upon an opportunity that you have in your portfolio right now. Without picking up the phone, and just using the information that you have on hand, use the Qualification Scorecard on the next page, go through your Qualification Questionnaire and fill in the quadrants.

Try to place a definitive "Yes" or "No" in each of the boxes by answering the following questions. For the binary system to work, you have to mark each box with a "1" for Yes" and a "0" for "No."

- ▶ Is there a perceived fit by the prospect between our products/services and their needs?
- ▶ Who are the Decision Makers and the Influencers and what is their decision-making process?
- ▶ When exactly does the prospect need to make the change and does it fit our time frame?
- ▶ Are there funds currently allocated for this project?

Date of Snapshot					
	(Y/N = 1/0)	(Y/N = 1/0)	(Y/N = 1/0)	(Y/N = 1/0)	(Y/N = 1/0)
Product Alignment (Match)					
Players					
Time Frame					
Funds					
Stage of Opp					

Use the Qualification Scorecard on every prospect you have. You may have a different outlook of the potential in your pipeline. You should revise your forecast or change your strategy in your territory scientifically.

What are the Results?

Many people have increased their closing ratios just by using these two Qualification tools. One of my clients sells Voice over IP systems to medium sized enterprises. Each system costs $55,000. After the 2-day Reinvent Sales Process boot camp, he applied his **Qualification Scorecard** intensively on every prospect. He increased his revenue by 32% in the next quarter.

How did he do this?

After his intensive boot camp, he re-qualified every prospect with the Reinvent Sales Process **ScoreCard**. Focusing on the Stage 3 Qualified and Stage 4 Committed, he set up meetings with them immediately. By zeroing in on these prospects, he knew what he needed to do to motivate them to move forward to the next Stage of the Buying Cycle. His **Scorecard** helped him to honestly classify them. He has internalized the skills since then. His sales manager was happy with this simple, proven method to reinvent the sales process for his sales team. It is all in the qualifying process. He is very positive about his sales results even in economic downturns.

Focus on the System

Many salespeople who have embraced this simple proven method, Reinvent Sales Process, have experienced similar remarkable results.

It is very simple and adaptable to any industry. You acquire the skill and ability to quickly assess and assign your prospects a Stage of Buying Cycle. When you couple your newly acquired skills with a focus on Stage 3 Qualified and Stage 4 Committed prospects, you improve your closing ratio.

Now, you need a system to synchronize all your sale activities at different stages of the buying cycle. Keep reading and completing the assignments and by the end of this part of the program, you will have developed your own system, from targeting your clients to generating loyal clientele.

Part IV -
Sales Activities Management

Introduction

Plan your work and work your plan. To be successful, you must plan your daily activities, review your monthly progress, and map out your strategic roadmap for the year. Your plan encourages you to be disciplined in your practice. Develop good working habits early in your sales career.

How to accelerate your prospect through his Stages of Buying Cycle? You learn about the underpinning importance of the Stages of Buying Cycle. What activities to perform to accelerate your prospects from one Stage to the next? What exactly you need to do at different stages of the buying cycle?

Activities ranging from marketing support, business development, sales, and customer service result in the generation of Lifelong customers. These activities facilitate the escalation from Stage 1 – *Indifferent* to final stage of *Closed/Sold.*

To be effective, you must perform each activity that *inspires* your prospect to take action. To inspire your prospects to move up the ladder of the Buying Cycle, you must motivate them to **act**, such as attend a seminar, respond to an email, request a white paper, accept an invitation to an event, make a phone call, participate in a webinar, or fill out a survey form. Then, you can measure that behaviour, or completed task objectively. Record these activities in your account history and monitor the progress.

Your prospects are experiencing constant changes in their business. To facilitate the process, you can provide them with proactive activities at different Stages of the Buying Cycle. You can label them in your arsenal as "Accelerators" or just "Sales Activities". These activities are best expressed in the examples in the following pages.

What Activities?

Performing Right Activities at the right Stage of Buying Cycle.

To facilitate positive change, you must perform these activities in the form of tools and techniques to activate the transition from one Stage of Buying Cycle to the next level.   Prospects at Stage 1 – *Indifferent* are usually unaware of their business problems due to industry legislation, or macroeconomic changes. They are indifferent to what is available in the market with respect to solution offerings. Several tangible tools are client surveys, technical white papers, case studies, webminars, or even business cards. You show and deliver value to your prospect. Each of these tools or techniques *motivates* your prospect to perform a specific *task* or *activity*.

For example, you can send your prospect a short survey to complete. The instruction is that they return it to you within 36 hours. By completing the survey and sending it back to you, they have completed the task or activity that you requested them to undertake. This activity is to encourage your prospect to take such an action by accepting a free gift or a special introductory offer to a new product offering.

Remember, it's not what people say that matters; it's what people *do*. Any completed activity can be accurately tracked and measured. To facilitate the buying process, inspire your prospect to complete the execution of a task. Each of these activities will help clarify where the prospect is in the Stages of Buying Cycle of making the change. More importantly, each activity will help them move up the ladder of transition.

Another awareness activity is an invitation to information webminars. You want to create awareness of potential problems to open minded prospects. From a supporting resources perspective, you have to seek assistance from your marketing department on this type of activity.

Assignment: *Write down some more examples of Activities in your selling world.*

Example: Share your resources in knowledge of the industry. Legislative Law – Worker's Compensation Regulations

North America Software Lumber Treaty between Canada and USA

Defining When to perform what activities:

1.   Activites for Stage 1 - Indifferent:

To create _awareness_ of potential business problems in their industry and encourage them to consider alternative ways of doing things. To generate new leads and opportunities.

Value-Added Information Sharing Activities:

(a) **Legislative Regulation Impact:**   Federal Security Commission imposes Sarbanes-Oxley Regulation in the United States and Bill 198 in Canada. These regulations demand that all publicly traded companies keep all email records for at least 7 consecutive years. This legislation creates a demand for email archival solutions. This impacts the growth of companies that produce disk drives and security software. It also affects companies like Cisco, NetIQ, and McFee that produce network security solutions in the hi-tech industry.

Data regulations imposed by the government will impact your prospect. Compliance with PCI and HIPPA are two other examples under this category. If your company provides disaster recovery services to the health care sector, you have a good reason to do it. You demonstrate your knowledge in the industry and you want to create the professional image of an expert.

(b) **Industry Standards:**   If your vertical target market is municipality government, by-laws, codes, and restrictions all have influence over how things are done. Consider the standards your clients must adhere to in order to stay in business legally or ethically. In the high-tech manufacturing industry, ISO Standards are well respected as the de facto standard of the manufacturing process. IEEE Standards in the telecommunications and engineering sector are recognized as the industry standard for communication protocol and 802.11 a/b/g, 802.11n, WiMAX in the wireless industry. Cisco, Alcatel-Lucent, ZTE, Hauwei are manufacturers for wireless switches and hubs. They all comply with the IEEE ("i-triple E") standards. These standards are usually established as one of the buying criteria in the high-tech industry.

(c) **Accredited Third Party Test Results:**   Accredited third party test results from well known and reputable sources are difficult to dispute. In the high-tech world, there are several third parties that may sway and influence those buying behaviors of your prospect.   CSA, ULC are accredited third parties that affect electronic equipment, such as computer servers, LCD display panels. They are the watchdogs for power safety. All electronic devices must be CSA approved for Canada, and ULC approved for USA.

(d) **Creative Marketing Strategies:**   In the hi-tech industry, printer companies promote their new printers at attractive prices while they recuperate the return on their investment in printer accessories that are purchased in the long run. This is also known as the "razor & razor blade" marketing strategy. If your prospect is in the consumable business, they may be interested in your views of marketing. You build your trusting relationship from here. You care for their business.

(e) **Social Networking:** Facebook.com, YouTube.com create a movement in social networking. In the business world, there are emerging companies that specialize in professional connections. Create your BLOG within your own website. Or simply join Linkedin.com, or Plaxo.com.

(f) **Referral from your Lifelong Customer:**   Ask for referrals from your lifelong customers. Your prospect will listen to your message if you are referred to them by one of their peers. If the referral is someone that is respected, you have a higher probability of meeting with your prospect. It beats a cold call to your prospect. A referral from the CIO of Weyhaeuser Ltd. to another CIO at Georgia Pacific Forestry Product Ltd. will open the doors for you. You can shorten your sales cycle.   The referral carries credibility and validation to your new prospect. Be proactive in your utilization of Social Influence by asking your Client-for-Life for referrals and letters of endorsement.

These are just a sample of activities. Use your creativity to come up with your own list that you can work with your Stage 1 - Indifferent prospects.

Formats of these messages/activities:

There are many formats to exchange information. You can communicate in the form of emails, phone calls, personal hand written notes, social networking gathering, event participation or even social dialogues in elevators. Use your imagination. The objective is to keep you on your prospect's radar.

2. Accelerating to Stage 2 - Interested

These activities trigger your prospects to take action. They are designed to increase your prospect's interest level and inspire them to move from Stage 1 - Indifferent to Stage 2 - Interested.

The following activities are illustrations that are commonly used in the information technology industry.

(a) <u>Webminars</u>: This media is getting more popular with the technology industry to educate prospects on the benefits of using their solutions.

(b) <u>White Paper</u>: White Paper serves the purpose of educating the prospect and offers ideas, proven models to enlighten the prospect about the potential use of their technology. Case Studies on the other hand are generic proof statements and stories in similar industry sectors. Prospects take action to download these documents. Quite often, the participants have to register before they can download the documentation. These cues will activate the mind to hook this new knowledge on to other information for future reference. It may inspire your prospect to jot down the information or physically file it away for future use. You should earn his permission to provide his contact information for a follow up call or email.

(c) <u>Advertising</u>: Advertising can inspire your Stage 4 – *Committed* prospect to take action. For an example, your prospect reads an ad in the paper for a new All-In-One Color LaserJet Printer for sale. The multi-functional printer will save him desk space, reduce his cost of printing, and combine all faxing, and color printing, scanning functions in one single machine. He has been inspired to visit a dealer's showroom sometime soon.

(d) **Brochures**: Companies spend trillions of dollars on marketing collateral every year. A carefully crafted brochure, a one-page information sheet, a best practice white paper, or a case study may not make the phone ring, but it will trigger the prospect with memory cues.

(e) **Statistical Evidence - "Proof" Statement**: Accredited third party evidence, recognized by your prospect as a respected source of trusted information, is a powerful tool. Use statistics that are backed by an authorized source. Statistics and survey reports conducted by the Gartner Group, Yankee Group, IDC, or Forrester Research, are strong validation of your technology, market trends, or rate of Buying Cycle of your high-tech solutions.

(f) **Testimonials:** It's important to have an enthusiastic testimonial in your introduction promotional material or marketing collateral to appeal to prospects at Stage 2 - *Interested* and Stage 3 - *Qualified*. Have a compelling, 20-word testimonial from a client stating how your service has improved his business life. This is a synopsis of "what other people say about their experience with your company".

(g) **Case Studies**: People at Stage 3 - *Qualified* have a timeline yet they may or may not have a budget in place. They usually want to see case studies or histories with subtle emotionally arousing testimonials and facts. Decision Makers at Stage 2 - *Interested* respond best to short one-page case studies and they frequently request more in-depth documents. This is a detailed loyal customer testimonial outlining the defined problems, thought process, decision making process, and the final outcome, *plus* their pleasant successful experience with your company.

(h) **Letters of Reference**: Prospects at Stage 2 -

Interested and Stage 3 - *Qualified* seek credibility validation. They respond well to letters of reference. Credibility relieves the risk factor and anxiety. Asking for a Letter of Reference should be part of your sales process. It should not be an after thought exercise. The sales process is not complete until the Letter of Reference is proudly displayed in your office, and may be included as part of your presentation.

(i) <u>Success Stories</u>: People like to hear "war stories" and "success stories" that illustrate triumphs over adversity. Prepare and arm yourself with true success stories. Your prospects align themselves with success. They want to be winners when they buy the solution from you. Give your prospect the confidence and comfort level that "someone like him has succeeded with your company". Your company has experiences in solving similar problems at other companies. This is the peace of mind your prospect is looking for in your company's successful track record.

Tip! *Apply these activities to inspire your prospects that are at either Stage 1–Indifferent or Stage 2 - Interested to move to the next Stage of Buying Cycle. Establish your company as the expert with domain expertise in the industry.*

Your activities in Stage 2 - Interested

To increase your prospect's awareness by providing valuable information that will enhance the level motivation.

Assignment: *List some of your marketing collateral and selling tools. Which of these incorporate "awareness", "demand creation" activities?*

Example: Business Card, corporate brochures, line card (computer reseller), product comparison chart)

_____

_____

_____

_____

_____

_____

_____

_____

_____

_____

_____

_____

_____

_____

_____

_____

_____

3.   **Assessment Tools for Stage 2 Interested and Stage 3 Prospects.**

To review and reappraise your sales activities at this Stage. To assess the status before embarking on additional activities.

It is important to review your sales activities during your sales campaign. Your prospect goes through his thought process. Here are additional tools that you can utilize in this transitional period.

(a) <u>Surveys & Scoring</u>:   Industry research groups such as Gartner Group, Forrester Research, and Yankee Group, produce market research reports and surveys on a regular basis. They have established credibility and are well respected in the information technology industry. If they present affirmative scoring of your offerings, you earn instant credibility through this type of third party endorsement for your company.

Decision Makers at Stage 2 - *Interested* are seeking information that will provide them with some insight. They are going through the assessment process of the pros and cons of many offerings. They analyze their business situation and examine all possible "what if" scenarios. They will be open to completing a short assessment questionnaire at this juncture. The objective of such an exercise is to determine if they should move forward with their problem solving efforts. The assessment questionnaire should be between five and eight questions in length for people who you identify as being at Stage 2 - *Interested.*

(b) <u>Assessment Questionnaire & Analysis</u>:   It is absolutely mandatory to conduct a fact finding Assessment with your prospect. Therefore, you should have a short assessment questionnaire (or survey) prepared for your Stage 2 – *Interested* prospects.

For a Stage 3 – *Qualified* and Stage 4 – *Committed* prospect, you should design a more detail Review Assessment questionnaire with nine to eighteen points. These short assessment surveys should take no more than five to ten minutes to complete. The Review Assessment should take no more than 20 minutes for the Stage 3 and 4 prospects.

(c) **Paid Assessment, Diagnostic & Analysis:**   Prospects at Stage 3 - *Qualified* are willing to invest to thoroughly investigate and research a suitable solution. Some may even pay for it to minimize their obligation to the company. These engagements are similar to pilot projects, proof of concept, or a trial/evaluation. The deliverable of such paid engagement can be in the format of a report of analysis of data, in-depth interviews and independent research. Decision Makers expect a complete understanding of their situation and if there is a match with your recommended offerings. This offering can be part of your "Whole" product. Some IT companies label this engagement as "professional services" or "Consulting Services". Your consulting team defines the scope of work and delivers the services as an independent study. This is a mini sales leading to the major opportunity. This small scale project carries a strategic value in your account management activities.

(d) **A Certified Test:**   In lieu of a paid Assessment Study or diagnostics, you can suggest a certified test on your solution in their operating environment. This is not a demo, rather it is a simulation. The purpose is to validate your offerings in their environment. The certified test may accelerate your prospect to the next Stages of Buying Cycle. One major computer manufacturer calls this exercise a "bake-off" if a competitive solution is also in the running.

These are proven toolsets that you can incorporate in your practice. Some companies have included these tools on their website in their Resource Library. You can encourage your prospects to complete a questionnaire online. You can follow up with a short telephone conversation to review their responses and provide them with a short analysis of their situation. There are many ways to apply these tools without perceived aggressiveness.

Helpful Hint: *Design your questionnaire with the terminology used in your target vertical market.*

Your current Assessment tools for evaluation to transition your prospect to the next level.

Assignment: *Write down a few examples that fit the Assessment. Identify those thoughtful reappraisals of the situation.*

_____

_____

_____

_____

_____

_____

_____

_____

_____

_____

4.   Moving Your Stage 3 - *Qualified* Prospect to Stage 4 - *Committed*.

To identify all relevant sales and promotional activities to accelerate your Stage 3 - *Qualified* prospect to the next level.

Stage 3 – *Qualified* prospects are important to your success. They have secured approved funding, found the match with your offerings to their problem, identified all players, and defined the timeline. This is the critical stage in the buying cycle and you must work hard to accelerate them to the next level.

(1) **Proposal**: This is the right time to prepare a proposal and present it to your prospect. You should not propose to them until your prospect is qualified. You should never do it before this stage. It is not just a quotation requested by your prospect. This is your opportunity to present your value and the total solution. You must demonstrate your understanding of their problem before offering a solution, your value-added services with a full support program. It is the whole product that your prospect should consider, and not just the price. This document differentiates you from your competitors. Proceed with care and diligence. If possible, present the proposal. Do not just put the proposal in the mail.

(2) **RFP (Request for Proposal)**: If you are dealing with government agencies, you have other regulatory process to work through. When you understand the buying process of your government account, you can assist them with all necessary technical and related information for their RFP preparation process. There is a lot of up front development activities before you arrive at the RFP process. If you do not know about this buying process, you should consult your mentor in your company to seek advice and guidance.

(3) **Presentation**: Once you complete the proposal, you should present it to the decision makers. You should follow the format

and logical approach of the proposal. Although presentation skills are not part of the scope of this WorkBook, you can consult other references on presentation skills. My sequel book on Applied Fundamentals will include a presentation section.

(4) **Systematic Follow up**: In most cases, you do not get a purchase order at the presentation. After the presentation, you must stay close to your prospect. Continue to use your *ScoreCard* to evaluate the sales campaign in your follow up activities. Assess your sales situation using your ScoreCard after every interaction with your prospect. Handle all objections and questions when they surface. You must be prepared to provide testimonials to reinforce the proposal.

Assignment: *Write down all the key components of the proposal.*

Example: Problem definition, solution offerings, support, pricing sections in a proposal.

---

5. Activities Applicable at Stage 4 - Committed to Stage 5 - Closed

To motivate your prospects to commit to your proposal, sign on the dotted line.

After your presentation to your Stage 3 - *Qualified* prospect, you want to accelerate him to Stage 4 – *Committed*. You enter the most vulnerable period of your sales campaign because your competitor has been watching. Your competitor has not sat idling. You must close this prospect before your competitor makes the move on you. If the commitment involves a sizable investment, you can apply one of the following techniques.

(1) *Purchase* **of an Assessment, or a Pilot Project**: Your Stage 3 – *Qualified* prospect is ready to invest BUT he is very cautious about such a major investment.   Since you have been using your *Scorecard* from Day 1, you know he is qualified. You understand the problem/solution match, identify the Time Frame, and confirm his funding allocation. At this point, you may suggest that he try a "Project Viability Test" with a small investment between 10 to 25 percent of the total cost. You want to take a small step before his considerable commitment. Use this approach when you are confident with the relationship.

"Pilot" is a term used frequently in the technology industry. Your prospect may be willing to invest a small percentage of the committed funding to validate the technology and your professional staff. It is logical for you to include the pilot project as part of the overall implementation schedule. For example, the pilot becomes the first phase of a new network infrastructure.

Your prospect knows how to mitigate his risk. For complex projects, your prospect wants to be sure if he is on the right track to succeed with you. A small investment in purchasing a pilot project demonstrates his level of commitment with you. It will prove your claims, credibility, ability, capacity and your promise to deliver. This is a small step but it shows commitment to buy from you.

(2) **The Cheque (Payment or deposit):** Writing a cheque is the ultimate expression of commitment. Your Stage 3 - *Qualified* prospect is willing to invest a relatively small percentage of the proposed investment if he witnesses a validated solution. Upon a successful completion of the validation, he can then confidently forecast the total financial investment. This small investment will minimize the risk and validate his judgment call. When he writes the cheque for the exploratory work to validate the solution, he demonstrates his commitment. The tools to acquire such a commitment are your Proposal, your Contractual Agreement and your Invoice.

(3) **Memo of Understanding (MOU) or a Letter of Intent (LOI):** These are instruments to demonstrate commitment before a final legal agreement is drawn up. The MOU can also serve the purpose of a proposal. It forms the premise of the legal contract.

Tip! *It is important to define the next step when the pilot succeeds as predicted.*

---

(4) **Provision of their Project Plan:** At the appropriate time, you should ask your Stage 3 - *Qualified* prospect for a copy of their project plan. When he approves and shows you the project plan, you receive a signal of their commitment to work with you. Otherwise, (depending on your relationship with the prospect), you may ask to see a copy of their action plan prior to responding to a Request for Proposal (RFP). The project plan is a formal document outlining their situation, their challenges, their needs, the budget, the people who need to be involved and the timeline. When they share with you this document, they demonstrate their trust in you and show they are prepared to partner with you.

It is prudent to enquire if they have such a plan on file at the outset. If they don't have one, you can offer to develop one for them. You can charge them to do the plan (i.e. the "paid"

Diagnostic or Assessment stated above).

(5) **Request Meeting with *all* of the Decision Makers**: This is a demonstration of commitment when your prospect agrees to a 45 to 90-minute meeting with all the Decision Makers in one room. You should request permission to present to the steering committee or the board of decision makers as a group. The purpose of such meeting is to present an in-depth Assessment report, your proposal, or a discussion of your recommended solutions. You have the opportunity to address all of their individual concerns and explore any hidden agendas in this meeting. When you meet with all decision makers individually, you must make sure that you keep the "dominant" decision maker abreast of your progress. Make him an ally and a supporter. By default, when your prospect officially introduces you to other decision makers, you are making progress.

(6) **Letter of Engagement**: This is comparable to a contract. For smaller project and management services for pilot projects, this document serves as a proposal and agreement. Use this document for validation of your proposed solution.

(7) **Contract**: This is the ultimate form of commitment. This contractual agreement is also the beginning of a new relationship. Your prospect becomes your customer. If one of the terms in your contract indicates a security deposit to proceed, don't forget to ask for the deposit cheque. You may need an official purchase order to complete the buying cycle. For government agencies and major enterprises you need an official purchase order.

Helpful Hint: Get sophisticated. When the Decision Maker is at Stage 4 - Committed or Stage 3 - Qualified, you want to deliver a Memorandum of Understanding (MOU) in their hands within 48 hours. This MOU gives you time to work on the official contract. It is important to understand the culture and buying pattern of your prospect. Use their terminology not yours.

---

(8) **Guarantees of Services:** Before your prospect signs the official contract, he will exhibit buyers' remorse syndrome. Your Stage 4 – *Committed* prospect needs reassurances that he is making the right decision with you. You must reinforce to him that his decision is the safe route to success. It is extremely important to prevent buyers' remorse behaviour. When you receive the purchase order, or a deposit cheque, you enter the new phase of a different relationship. He becomes your customer. There will be more hard work ahead of you to enhance this new relationship and make him a lifelong customer. Your "100% Satisfaction Guarantee" may take the pressure off your prospect.

(9) **Corporate Volume Discount:** Discounting is a give-and-take bargaining process. If you must offer a discount at the point of signing the contract, you should bargain for future volume commitment in exchange for a corporate discount or site license discount pricing schedule (for software license fee). In exchange for a volume discount, you can also solicit other commitment, such as becoming your reference account for good will, or volunteering as a beta site for new products, or a pilot site for future versions of your offerings.

Another approach to manage discount discussion is to offer credits in exchange for purchasing training courses, certification process, and new products. You can also negotiate special discounts on the basis of amending the technical specification to a slower processor, or slower hard disk array to meet their budget constraint.

Cutting price to meet a competitive bid is dangerous without any legitimate reasons. Your credibility will be challenged if you lower your price for no reason. You can leverage the approach of reducing the number of shipments. When you encourage your prospect to take more stock quantity per shipment, you can justify the discount as it is more attractive financially to their bottom line. Another incentive is to offer them a "preferred client status" to accelerate your customer relationship. You can also create "bundles" of categories of products, such as network switches, servers, hard disk arrays, and consulting services. This tactical approach will differentiate you from your competition as well. You must offer more value to your prospect to build a long term relationship with them instead of entering a pricing contest with your competition.

Accelerating to Stage 5 - Closed/Sold

To apply all activities to motivate your Stage 4 - *Committed* prospect to the next level --- Stage 5 - *Closed/Sold*.

Assignment: Write down some other examples of Commitment tools and techniques in your selling, marketing or client service world.

Examples: Memo of understanding, Letter of Intent, Letter of credit if you are dealing with an overseas prospect.

_____

_____

_____

_____

_____

_____

_____

Request For Proposal (RFP)

When you have no knowledge of an upcoming RFP (Request for Proposal), you will have a challenge at hand. Your competitor has been working the opportunity while you are busy pursuing other prospects. You have a decision to make if you should expense any effort on this opportunity. Your objective is to minimize any waste of resources to manage such perceived "opportunity". This is a judgment call on your part. Is this a strategic account that is part of your mandate assigned by your company?

When your prospect sends you an RFP (Request for Proposal), it doesn't mean that you are selected for the project. The first challenge you have is that you don't know their stage of the buying cycle. Unless you have been working with this prospect for a while, you have to map out a strategy and make a decision. A RFP may not provide you with all the information about this project. Crucial information, such as inclusion of project timeline, funding allocation, directory of decision makers, may not be available. The time frame for the submission of your response usually ranges from 4 weeks to 6 weeks. If the deadline of the submission is short, they probably made their selection. For example, if you are given 10 days to respond to a complex project design and you know nothing about this project in advance, your competitor is entrenched with the decision makers. This RFP is just a formality to meet the policy requirement of their organization.

If you decide to proceed, your immediate task is to establish the stage of their buying cycle. When they do not define a timeline, or their deadline is next year, you have time to categorize their Stage of Buying Cycle. You can then determine if this is a viable opportunity to pursue. There is a possibility that they are just in the process of information gathering (Stage 2 - *Interested*) and not at Stage 4 - *Committed*.

All government agencies send out a RFP to pre-qualified vendors because it is legislative requirement. They project an atmosphere of fairness and equity for all vendors. Quite often, your prospect knows exactly whom he is going to do business with. However, they must present the evidence of their due diligence to their stakeholders. Regardless of their motives, you must qualify the opportunity by identifying their Stage of Buying Cycle and all decision makers. Use your **Qualification Questionnaire** and **Qualification Scorecard** to help you to qualify the opportunity objectively. At times, you may not be given such an opportunity to discuss the project with the decision makers. Some organizations will post a "black out" period that all enquiries must be directed through the coordinator of the RFP. You are basically locked out if you didn't build any relationships with their decision makers. Make your decision and allocate your resources accordingly.

Helpful Hint: Government agencies post their RFP (Request for Proposals) at a public "bid" website portal in conjunction with the invitation process. If they adopt the policy of posting only, you will not get invited to bid on these projects. Register with your government's public bidding site so you get notification of any potential projects that fit your solution portfolios

---

Some companies' decision-making processes involve the issuance of an RFP. Your strategy is to get involved *early* in their buying cycle which is before the issuance of such an official document. During your first fact-finding meeting with your prospect, you must find out if they have an official bidding policy. If such a policy exists, you should strategically influence the buying behavior and assist him in defining the project criteria. Your expert input will carry significant impact on the content and intent of the RFP document. Hopefully, your prospect will include technical specifications that are unique to your company. This preparation work will pay dividend when the RFP document is officially released.

Request for Information (RFI) documents are good indications that you have a Stage 2 - *Interested* opportunity. Use your **Qualification Scorecard** and **Qualification Questionnaire** to confirm the Stage of Buying Cycle *before* prescribing the appropriate activities for your sales campaign.

Heads up! *When you receive a legitimate RFP from a Stage 4 Committed opportunity, you should take a step back if you know nothing about the opportunity.*

You still have a few things to do: Conduct a thorough Assessment, meet with all the Decision Makers. Then you are ready to submit your response to the "Request for Proposal" document. Be aware of the rules and regulations. Some organizations will not allow sales people to sell to their decision makers once the RFP is issued. Don't take chances and get in the door early. Help them with your unique specifications. When your unique specifications are included and highlighted in the RFP, you have a higher probability to win the project.

In some cases, your prospect has a legacy solution to their "perceived" problem. If your prospect's business-operating environment has changed due to new government regulations, he realizes that he "can't adapt to these changes with the current technology solution". He is looking for an improvement; otherwise he wouldn't have time to meet you. Your prospect is weighing his options and evaluating your solution for potentially replacing the existing solution.

How to help a Stage 4 - Committed prospect arrive at a positive behaviour over existing products and solution?

Assignment: Take a few moments to think of other tools, programs, bundling or creative tools. Use examples in your work place.

Example: Volume Discount Price List; Different product bundling; Referral Account status; End of life product stocking; Training, Certification Credit; Marketing Development funding; Manufacturer Year-end rebates

6.   Other business development Tools/activities:

To change the selling environment and scenarios to encourage your prospect to do something different

Sophisticated business developers and sales professionals understand the importance of a change of scenario when their prospect reaches Stage 4 - Committed. Some of the following activities will inspire them to move on to Stage 5 - Closed/Sold.

(1) <u>Social and Leisure Activities</u>: A change of scenery creates a more relaxed environment to build a long term relationship. Why do you think golf is such an important sport in the business world today? You have a captive audience's attention for four and a half hours. After 18 holes of relaxation, you and your prospect get to know each other better.

During your first fact finding meeting, you can find out if there is a common subject of interest between you and your prospect. There are many hobbies that people engage in during their leisure time. Golf is just one among many, such as skiing, tennis, photography, or mountain biking. Find this common denominator early when you want to build such a relationship.

For a social golf game, it is prudent *not* to discuss business on the course. It is considered impolite. If your prospect brings it up, you have the option of postponing the discussion to Hole 19. The golf game provides your prospect an opportunity to know you as a person rather than just as a sales professional. Your game will reveal your true character through this 18-hole exercise. You definitely will demonstrate your honesty at the end of the round as well when it comes to totaling your score of the day.

There is one particular hole where you can start a business discussion - the 19th. Do not discount this strategic position at the end of the round. You enter a different environment at the 19th hole.

If you don't golf, or choose not to, there are numerous alternatives that provide an environment for relationship building. These can include sailing, skiing, racket ball, tennis or any cultural events – any leisure activity that both you and you prospect can enjoy together. Going to a musical, a play, or an opera are some examples of a change of environment to help build a relationship between you and your prospect.

Charity, community involvement, your children's soccer game, and music concerto provide opportunities for your prospect to get to know you better. The Leadership Program at United Way consists of senior executives of major corporations. Your contribution to this program will help to build your own reputation in the community. Junior Achievement, Board of Trade Mentoring programs and other positive circles with good causes are tools for Environmental Control. Participate and contribute to society. It is good for the soul and your career.

(2) **Corporate Site Visit**: Corporate visits should be part of your sales cycle, especially with major projects. When your prospect accepts your invitation to visit your corporate head office, you impress your prospect with the strength and ethical culture of your company. Your prospect is not just buying the product from you; rather he will build a long term relationship with your company. When your executive team welcomes your prospect, they demonstrate their commitment to support your prospect. You should recruit a senior executive internally as the "corporate sponsor" for this prospect. Build a bridge between your two organizations at the executive level. There is some preparation work for this event. Your executive sponsor must be briefed prior to the visit. He can reinforce to your prospect the support, and the future direction of your company to mitigate the risk for your prospect when your solution is adopted.

(3) **Lifelong Customer Reference Site Visit**: This type of visit validates your solution that has been implemented in an

environment similar to that of your prospect. You must be cautious if your Lifelong Customer is a competitor to your prospect. When your North American prospect accepts an invitation to visit a reference site in Germany, you know you are very close to success. It is an investment on their part and it is also part of their due diligence process. You must brief your Lifelong Customer prior to the visit accordingly. Your customer becomes your ambassador.

Apply this powerful activity early with Stage 4 - **Committed** prospects. Take them to the site of a Lifelong Customer. Invite your Lifelong Customer to host such a visit. Give your Lifelong Customer an opportunity to boast about their success since using your product within their organization. Let them demonstrate their success using their statistical data on performance improvement, impact on productivity, operational cost savings, increases in revenues and profits. They are proud of their achievements since using your solution. If the improvement is also reflected by a positive increase in their stock value, they should point that out too. The bottom line is that you are part of the success story and they are proud to tell the story.

Helpful Hint: *Be careful. Take a prospect to a site visit after you've conducted an in-depth assessment. The site visit has to be relevant, and not a waste of time.*

The length of such visits impacts your preparation and activities. If it is only a one-day event, ensure that you have a luncheon arranged during the event. You want to include as many decision makers as possible in these events. It gives you the opportunity to assess your prospect's Stage of Buying Cycle. Come prepared with your proposal, the contractual agreement and the invoice, just in case they respond positively and want to sign the deal there and then.

If this is a multiple day event, arrange social activities for your guests. You must prepare for it and attend to every single detail. If you have an internal team that is responsible for such executive site visits, you can delegate such planning activities to them. They will have more resources and local knowledge for such visits. If you have other participants from your own organization, make sure you brief them on the background of the prospect, their expectations, and the objective of the visit. Demonstrate your leadership as a gracious host.

Tips!   *Site Visits are very important in closing deals. You must gauge your progress with the prospect and your own diligence. If you have not assessed the Stage of Buying Cycle, you will be shooting a shotgun blind-folded. You must be prepared. Use your ScoreCard persistently. Your corporate executive team follows your direction on such a visit. Don't make them look silly. Otherwise, your own corporate career is at stake too. Your corporate executives measure your performance at these events. Come prepared. Coach your internal participants. Coach your Lifelong Customer as if they were part of your corporate visit. Golf games at Pebble Beach Golf and Country Club are very expensive. This is your investment too. Get the most return on the investment.*

Other Business Development Tools/Activities.

Assignment: Write down some other examples of Environmental Control in your selling world.

Example: Lunch

Example: 18+1 hole golf game

_____

_____

_____

7.   Activities of Reinforcement – Post Sales Service

To reward your newly minted customer for positive behaviour.

It's absolutely paramount that you reward your new customer to appreciate their support and business. What you present to them as a "thank you" must be done tastefully and professionally. Here are some examples:

(1) **Small Token Gift**: You should present a gift of appreciation to your new customer, Stage 5 - *Closed/Sold* after the contract is signed, sealed and delivered. Some organizations have rules for accepting gifts, especially in the case of government agencies. They may have a policy on the value of gifts, for example gifts are not to exceed $20. There are unspoken rules about gifts in some organizations. Some Fortune 500 companies limit their gifts to not exceed $75. Government employees cannot accept gifts at all during RFP/bidding period. They may accept small token gifts if they are less than $75 in value. Lunches, dinner and a friendly golf game are acceptable. You must also check with your own company about the gift giving policy.

A small token present is an acceptable etiquette as it is a sign of appreciation. When he signs the deal, not before, show your appreciation with a dinner and celebrate the beginning of a long-term relationship.

(2) **Entertainment**: You must ensure that the reward corresponds with the desired task or activity. For example, you probably wouldn't buy a prospect a $500 dinner that includes very expensive Chateau La Tour Bordeaux. Expensive dinner is a double-edged sword. It may give your prospect the wrong impression about your

company and yourself. Get to know your prospect first before you embark on the change of scenario strategy. Understand his personal traits, his taste and character.

It is inappropriate to offer a lavish, luxurious gift to your prospect early in the Stage of Buying Cycle. When a particular behavior has not been completed by your prospect, your act of gift giving sometimes can be construed as a pay-off, a bribe, or an obligation to do business. Some prospects feel uncomfortable, and more importantly, it may be illegal. When you design your sales tool sets and perform your sales activities, you must know the culturally acceptable behaviour expected in each country, industry or the company.

(3) **Under Promise & Over Deliver Motto**: When your performance exceeds your customer's expectations, you retain your customer without shaving your profit margin. You should set the expectation level and define milestones in advance. Your next impressive performance is to deliver ahead of schedule. You pave the road for future business, and earn the right to ask for referrals and testimonials.

(4) **Professional Etiquette - Respect for Time**: There are many professional etiquette in business. This subject is out of the scope of this Workbook. The most obvious and sometimes ignored etiquette is the appreciation of your prospect's time. Be punctual to all meetings. Try to be 10 minutes ahead of schedule. It will give you time to relax before the meeting. At the beginning of every meeting, you should confirm with your prospect the amount of time he has allocated for you. Adhere to your time schedule with your agenda. If you can, wrap up early and set the date for the next meeting.

Activities of Reinforcement - Post Sales Service

Assignment: Make a list of little gifts for your very busy Stage 4 - Committed prospects and thank them for all of those little incremental steps they've taken to eventually do business with you. How else can you reward

your clients and prospects at the Stage 4 Committed, Stage 5 Sold &
Serving and Lifelong Customer?

Example: The gift of time

_____

_____

_____

_____

_____

_____

_____

_____

_____

_____

_____

_____

_____

8. Activites for Extending Relationships

To do more by enlisting other team members to help.

Stage 4 - *Committed* prospects have the highest "slippage rate". It is mainly due to your competition and buyer uncertainty. You must maintain regular communication with them at this stage. You must be available to answer any questions quickly or delegate it to your pre-sales team members. This instant response reinforces your prospect's perception of your company. You must demonstrate your commitment to take care of your prospects, before and after the sales. Please remember your competition is standing by. They wait and wish for mishaps in your sales campaign with your prospects. Your competitors will make them available to your prospects, and connect with them. Don't fall asleep or blink, especially when your prospect arrives at Stage 4 - *Committed*.

Communication technology is helping you to maintain constant contact with your prospect. Smart Cell phones, personal digital assistance (PDA) devices, Blackberry, iPhone, take care of your impromptu connections. These intelligent devices also help you to organize your day-to-day activities. You are connected anywhere, anytime. Your internal resources should be available promptly. Your pre-sales engineering support team and your post-sales service team are important parts of your sales team. They can help in maintaining constant contact with your prospects and customers.

Activities for Extending Relationships

Assignment: Write down other examples of helping relationship tools and techniques that you would like to provide to your clients and prospects in your organization.

Example: Client Service Help Desk

Example: Pre-sales systems engineer

Example: Chief financial Officer in your company

_____

_____

_____

_____

Summary of Sales Activities to facilitate Positive Change

There are many activities that you perform during the complete buying cycle, from Stage 1 – *Indifferent* to Stage 5 – *Closed/ Sold*. We provide you with a sample of proven activities for these stages of the buying cycle. You should explore, experiment, and augment this list. When you do your assignment in this section, you would probably identify your own tool sets that your company already provides. With all the tools, you should have a personal sales plan completed by now. Use a 3-Ring Binder, a recipe box, or the disk drive of your laptop to maintain the updated record of your prospects in your pipeline. You have technology devices to maintain your communications with your prospects and customers. Give yourself time to internalize this simple process to Reinvent Your Sales Process. You will be successful in your sales career.

Do not stop here. Keep learning new tools, further your education and seek coaching from your manager.

Congratulations!

You have come this far. You have the blue print to create your own Personal Strategic Sales Plan. You have the tools to perform your personal review. I offer e-coaching services, sales assessment and advisory services to my clients. Send your email to **byan@fwin.ca** directly and I will reply to your request as soon as I am available. I am confident that you will be successful in overachieving your goals and objectives when you reinvent your sales process.

Summary of Worksheets

Customize Your Own Personal Sales Activities Plan

Stage 1 Indifferent	Stage 2 Interested

Stage 3 Qualified	Stage 4 Committed

Stage 5 Closed/Sold	Stage 6 Lifelong Customer

Qualification Scorecard Matrix

Date of Snapshot					
	(Y/N = 1/0)	(Y/N = 1/0)	(Y/N = 1/0)	(Y/N = 1/0)	(Y/N = 1/0)
Product Alignment (Match for Solution)					
Players					
- CEO					
- CFO					
- CIO					
* Influencers					
Time Frame					
Funds					
Stage of					
Opportunity					

ABOUT THE AUTHOR:

Ben Yan has spent over three decades in sales, marketing experience, equity financing for technology start up companies as an entrepreneur, and years in the corporate world for manufacturers Sun Microsystems and Hewlett Packard. He still practices the HP way in his traveling and business ventures. He was most recently the CEO & President of Sino Fibre Communication Inc, a publicly listed NASD company. He spent an extensive amount of time in China on merger and acquisition projects. He also sits on the boards of several technology companies. Some of these companies had gone public on NASDAQ and TSX. Ben is a frequent speaker at sales professional entrepreneur conferences. He is a visiting professor on International Marketing at the Sauder School of Business MBA program, and consults on sales process design, commercialization of technology products, sales force re-engineering, and client relationship management. Ben performs HealthCheck for technology companies and has expanded his practice to China, the fastest growing economy in the world. He also conducts sales reengineering workshops, product commercialization planning and distribution channel management workshops for growth companies globally.

He can be reached at byan@fwin.ca